NOT 'DAFFODILS' AGAIN! — TEACHING POETRY 9-13

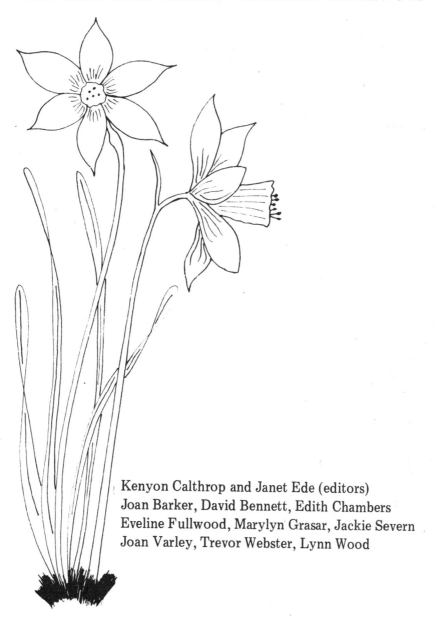

Kenyon Calthrop and Janet Ede (editors)
Joan Barker, David Bennett, Edith Chambers
Eveline Fullwood, Marylyn Grasar, Jackie Severn
Joan Varley, Trevor Webster, Lynn Wood

LONGMAN
1984

Title page drawing by Jackie Severn

Typeset by Linda Harvey,
56 Offley Road, London SW9 OLS

This title, an outcome of work done for the
Schools Council before its closure, is published
under the aegis of the School Curriculum
Development Committee, Newcombe House,
45 Notting Hill Gate, London W11 3JB.

Published by Longman Group UK Ltd
Printed in Great Britain by
Longman Resources Unit
62 Hallfield Road
Layerthorpe
York YO3 7XQ

CONTENTS

FOREWORD

'Poetry begins in delight'

This book, which deals practically with the teaching of poetry, is first and foremost an expression of delight. As the authors point out, for many children and adults there has been little or no delight gained from poetry. This book seeks to alter that by encouraging readers to share in the delight that the contributors and their pupils have so obviously experienced, and then to use that feeling of delight as a starting-point for their own teaching of poetry.

Much of the Schools Council's recent curriculum development has been organized in five programmes. Programme 2, of which this study is part, has aimed to help teachers with their professional development. The programme has based its work on certain key principles all of which are shown clearly in this book. Not 'Daffodils' Again! focuses on classroom practice; it gives examples of teachers appraising their own practice and then undertaking classroom action-research into their own teaching. Above all it embodies the belief of the programme that working in partnership with others helps teachers in their professional development.

As an educational text this book is unusual in that it does not seek to offer ready-made solutions to problems. Instead it gives samples of 'thoughtful, usually effective, but not always perfect poetry teaching'. These samples are followed by sections designed to encourage teachers to pinpoint and then explore for themselves some of the issues arising.

Although it is hoped that this book will be extremely valuable to those in initial training, as well as to those with some experience of poetry teaching, it should be remembered that just as it 'begins in delight', so it should also end in delight.

DON COOPER
Programme Director

v

ACKNOWLEDGEMENTS

We would like to thank all the people who helped to make this project and this book possible. These include advisers, secretaries and educational technicians. We received financial and practical support from the Schools Council, Derbyshire College of Higher Education and Trent Polytechnic.

We are grateful also for the support and co-operation of heads and colleagues in the following schools and for permission to include their pupils' poems:

Brockwell Junior School, Chesterfield, Derbyshire
Christ Church C. E. Primary School, Chesterfield, Derbyshire
Cromford C. E. Primary School, Cromford, Derbyshire
George Spencer Comprehensive School, Stapleford, Nottingham
Joseph Whitaker Comprehensive School, Rainworth, Notts.
Milford Junior School, Clifton, Nottingham
Priory R. C. Primary School, Eastwood, Nottingham
Radcliffe Junior School, Radcliffe-on-Trent, Nottingham.

Above all we are grateful for the sympathetic advice and support of John Paine, Schools Council field officer for the East Midlands.

All these people have supported us wholeheartedly, often at inconvenience to themselves.

Thanks are due to the following for permission to reproduce copyright material (full sources are listed in Appendix A):

Penguin Books Ltd. for 'Hard Cheese' by Justin St. John
David Higham Associates for 'Cat' by Eleanor Farjeon, and 'My Mother Saw a Dancing Bear' and 'What Has Happened to Lulu?' by Charles Causely
The Society of Authors, on behalf of the copyright holder Mrs Iris Wise, for 'The Shell' by James Stephens
Ian Serraillier for 'Miss Tibbles' by Ian Serraillier
Richard Rieu for 'Cat's Funeral' by E. V. Rieu
André Deutsch for 'My Dad's Thumb' by Michael Rosen
Fontana Paperbacks for 'My Party' by Kit Wright
Andrew Penwarden for 'The Great Gulls' by Andrew Penwarden
Macmillan Publishers Ltd. for 'Flannan Isle' by W. W. Gibson
Karl Fletcher for 'Cat' by Karl Fletcher
Faber and Faber Ltd. for 'Hawk Roosting' by Ted Hughes and 'Follower' by Seamus Heaney

Margaret and Jack Hobbs for 'Brave New World' by Spike Milligan
Allison and Busby Ltd. for 'A Case of Murder' by Vernon Scannell
Chatto and Windus Ltd. for 'The Apple Raid' by Vernon Scannell
Gregory Harrison for 'Posting Letters' by Gregory Harrison
Margaret Greaves for 'Stray Kitten' by Margaret Greaves.

Every effort has been made to trace and acknowledge the holders of copyright in
material included in this book. In order that any omissions may be rectified at the
earliest opportunity, Schools Council Publications would be glad to hear from anyone
who has not been contacted.

PROJECT MEMBERS

Joan Barker

After bringing up her two children, Joan Barker returned to teaching at Radcliffe-on-Trent Primary School in a large village on the outskirts of Nottingham where she has taught for the last 8 years. She is Language Consultant in the school and holds the O. U. Reading Development Diploma. She has a wide range of interests and is very involved in in-service work in her area.

David Bennett

Before moving to Nottinghamshire, where he is Head of English at an 11-16 urban comprehensive of 900 pupils, David Bennett was a teacher/librarian in Avon. He is a regular contributor to the School Bookshop publication Books for Keeps and frequently lectures on matters related to children's literature and the teaching of English. In 1981 he formed the Nottinghamshire Children's Literature Group and edited its first publication in the summer of 1982. He is married with two sons and lives in Derbyshire.

Kenyon Calthrop

Kenyon Calthrop has taught English in primary and secondary modern schools and in a college of education. At present he is Senior Lecturer in English in the School of Education at Trent Polytechnic. He recently spent a year overseas as a Visiting Fellow in Australia. He is the author/editor of a number of books for schools and about teaching, and General Editor of the 'Literature for Life' series for Arnold-Wheaton.

Edith Chambers

Edith Chambers has taught in secondary and junior schools and is at present Deputy Head in a Derbyshire junior school. Her first love is music, but literature follows a close second. She has always encouraged the writing of poetry and some of her children's poetry was read and discussed at education conferences in Canada. She has conducted various women's choirs, sings herself in a Sheffield choir and enjoys weekend music making and summer courses.

Janet Ede

After teaching English in a number of secondary schools, Janet Ede joined the English department of Derbyshire College of Higher Education, where she is now a senior lecturer in English and Warden of the Language and Reading Centre. She is particularly interested in children's literature and children's language development. In 1981 she published Talking, Listening and Learning (Longman) with Jack Williamson, which is concerned with children's spoken language.

Eveline Fullwood

Eveline Fullwood is married with one son and until recent early retirement was Deputy Head at Cromford C. E. School — a rural primary school in the historic Arkwright village. She now devotes her time to singing with the Derbyshire Singers, needlework and soft toy making. She always enjoyed poetry teaching and found inspiration for the children in the varied activities and occupations of the village.

Marylyn Grasar

Marylyn Grasar teaches at Priory R. C. Primary, a small school in Eastwood, Nottinghamshire, home of D. H. Lawrence. She works mainly in the infant department but also undertakes some language teaching with junior pupils, and is particularly interested in the relevance and value to children of poetry written for adults. She is a member of her local W.E.A. branch, and is involved in the promotion of adult education for the physically handicapped.

Jackie Severn

Jackie Severn, a Southerner by birth, ventured north of Watford Gap only to train as a teacher, but fell in love with the Midlands and decided to stay! She has taught art for nine years, English for four years, and has recently become a Deputy Year Tutor. Aside from teaching, her interests include badminton, cycling, books, books and books (. . . and two beautiful black felines called Sydney and Mellie.)

Joan Varley

Joan Varley has taught at Brockwell Junior School in Derbyshire since 1966, where she was given responsibility for the library and resources, and then for art, craft and display throughout the school. She often attends courses in art and does much of her writing while accompanying her husband on fishing and rugby trips.

Trevor Webster

Before returning to his native Nottinghamshire, where he is second in the English Department at an 11-18 comprehensive school, Trevor taught at a similar school in the old West Riding of Yorkshire. His poetic interests include the works of Berryman, Yeats and Maclean, and folk song.

Lynn Wood

Lynn Wood has been teaching in primary schools for eleven years and has experience in teaching children from nursery age up to top juniors. She is at present a Community Teacher on a large council estate in Nottingham, having previously held a special post for art and crafts. She is interested in outdoor pursuits, including youth hostelling and travel abroad.

Note: The names of pupils whose work is discussed, or quoted from, have been changed.

I. WHAT'S WRONG?

Poetry has had bad luck. It has suffered a double misfortune: neglect where it most needs attention and concern where it is best left alone.

'Poetry begins in delight' . . . With young children, above all, our rightful concern is with this delight.[1]

The Schools Council Programme 2 Project, Teaching Poetry 9-13, took shape from the working experience of the two project leaders with students in initial teacher training, teachers on in-service courses and children in schools. For a high proportion of these, children and adults, there was little or no delight to be gained from poetry.

If pressed, many adults might remember one or two poems from their school days. Wordsworth's 'Daffodils' would be high on the list, because many have been forced to learn it. It is only fair to say that in some cases what has initially been seen as enforced study gives some joy in its later recall. But very few — an exceptional few — have read, voluntarily, much twentieth-century poetry, and the lesson 'Poetry' which occasionally appears on primary timetables is an ordeal for many teachers. One experienced primary teacher described how, in the course of twenty-six years of teaching, she only encountered one student who <u>asked</u> to include poetry in his timetable, and who demonstrated a willingness to share that enthusiasm with children.

Faced with a curriculum based largely on the acquisition of 'knowledge' and 'skills', many teachers are insecure when confronted by a poetry lesson.

> The anxiety to pin the meaning down, to explain words, to take the class on a guided tour through the poem, enlivening it with metaphor hunts and simile chases, inexorably takes over. Worry about the rightness, both of a poem's meaning and of our teaching method, predominates, and the worry is conveyed to the children so that the classroom ambiance of poetry becomes one of anxiety at a difficult problem with hidden rules rather than one of enjoyment of a well-wrought object.[2]

Very few poems lend themselves to 'knowledge' as experienced by the knower in some subject areas, and once the relatively straightforward matters of poetic technique have been explained, many students and teachers feel themselves floundering when asked about the purpose of reading poetry to children. What is not <u>felt</u>, as well as <u>understood</u>, by the adult reader is not easily discussed with children. Some teachers, too, are wary of the emotional depths they sense beneath the surface meaning of poems, which evoke responses and emotions in themselves and their pupils that are not easily expressed in the classroom.

Further indications point to a decline in poetry work in schools and other educational institutions. David Holbrook has recently drawn attention to the twelve brief paragraphs in the Bullock Report[3] which are concerned with poetry, in a whole chapter devoted to literature. The tone of the report at this point is critical of current practice and is concerned with the lack of good poetry anthologies in schools and the need for more awareness of contemporary poetry. Mention is made of the dangers of subsuming poetry under a thematic approach; seen as equally dangerous is an over-emphasis on the analytical approach, particularly in O-level and CSE work. We are told that 'Poetry has great educative power,' but very little positive help is given to the classroom teacher about ways in which he can gain confidence in teaching in an area of work which generates uncertainty and unease.

Although the case for teaching poetry was put forcefully and with great distinction by Marjorie Hourd over thirty years ago,[4] there has been little or no curriculum development in this area, and the number of books devoted to poetry teaching published in the last decade compares very unfavourably with the rest of the 'English' curriculum. There are, doubtless, deep-seated and complex cultural reasons for this state of affairs, as Peter Abbs has discussed.[5] But one result is that poetry is taught badly in our schools or not at all.

Michael Benton, who with his brother Peter has edited a number of widely used anthologies, such as Touchstones and Watchwords, notes in an excellent short article that:

> Handling Poetry is the area of the primary/middle school curriculum and the secondary English curriculum where teachers feel most uncertain about their knowledge, most uncomfortable about their methods, and most guilty about both.[6]

Yet, on the positive side, the desire to remedy the situation is obviously there, on the part of teachers, trainee teachers and advisers. In-service courses and conferences on aspects of poetry are invariably well supported because teachers so clearly need help in this aspect of classroom work.

The Schools Council Programme 2 Project, Teaching Poetry 9-13, was developed as a result of the work of the co-editors with students on initial and in-service training courses. With limited funds and time available the 9-13 age-range seemed a good starting-point for a number of reasons:

1.   It is an age range where children are still at a formative stage and relatively unaffected by the pressures of external examinations or the traumas of adolescence.

2.   The broad and flexible curriculum of the good primary school provides an interesting base from which poetry teaching can be developed.

3.   The 9-13 age-range involves both primary and secondary schools and also includes middle schools where these exist.

The relatively short life of the project (one year plus dissemination) also placed constraints on the number of schools which could be drawn into the work, and it was therefore decided to limit the participating schools to eight, trying to effect a balance between primary and secondary schools. The limitations of time and scope precluded an examination of the state of poetry teaching in general, and it was decided to limit the range of schools to those where good practice was already known to be taking place. The teachers

involved were those with a particular interest in poetry, already teaching poetry successfully in their own classrooms.

Our hope was that we should set up a programme of the kind described in the opening paragraph of the Schools Council Programme 2 information leaflet, and based on the
notion of action-research, whose philosophy is that: 'activities should focus on the individual teacher's classroom work; that teachers work best on problems they have helped to
identify; and working in partnership with other teachers, with LEAs, with further and
higher education institutions and with other agencies, helps teachers in their professional
development.'

It became clear at the first meeting that, while teachers were concerned with examin-
ing and developing their own classroom practice and taking the opportunity to reflect on
what they were doing, they saw as one of their main aims the need to develop in-service
resources for other teachers. It was suggested that in order to achieve this important aim
and offer practical support to other teachers, a written report should include some of the
following:

1. Lists of poems appropriate for different age groups

2. Sources of poems

3. Suggestions as to ways in which individual poems might be presented and
    developed in the classroom

4. An indication of the wide range of responses we might encourage children to
    make to the poetry they had read

5. Appropriate methods of evaluating children's responses

6. A discussion of a rationale for poetry teaching

7. A consideration of the relationship of poetry and wider aspects of the
    curriculum.

It was decided that where possible the report should be supported by slides and videos
showing classroom practice.

During the course of the year, from the inception of the project, the project leaders
were able to visit teachers in their schools, in some cases to share directly in the teaching
process, and to discuss the progress of the work. It was heartening, in a number of cases,
to see members of staff (in some instances whole schools) drawn into the project so that
it became possible to see the beginnings of the curriculum change and development taking
place in a very positive way.

It has become clear that, while the project was a necessarily limited piece of work
within a small budget, it has had more effect in schools than had originally been envisaged.
Just what the effect had been in schools was revealed at a meeting in the spring term when
project members arrived loaded with art work, books and children's writing. It was a
wonderful display and demonstrated just what could be achieved by pupils, given the
guidance of a very professional group of teachers becoming increasingly confident in what
they were doing. Project members had been chosen originally because of their interest
and enthusiasm for poetry, and this display seemed to emphasize the expertise of the
group and underlined the wealth of ideas and resources which were available for sharing
with others.

What had originally been planned as a final report for project members and staff in
their schools became instead a report for national publication. The careful records

teachers had kept of their teaching of individual poems from Chapter II of this book, and their views on wider aspects of poetry work constitute Chapter III. Chapter IV presents two personal views of the meaning of poetry in individual lives.

The project has given pleasure to teachers, pupils, parents and project leaders. Now is the time to share that pleasure with others and to move some way towards fulfilling one of the main aims of making a positive contribution to initial and in-service training. To do this, we, the adults, have had to face the difficult task of organizing our ideas in writing, and in doing so have experienced something of the frustrations felt by our students and pupils when we ask them to write. It will have been worth it if, for more teachers, students and pupils, poetry can 'begin in delight'.

II. 'THE POEM TOOK OVER'

Some Individual Accounts of Poetry Teaching

The Snow Goose

A pale shape soars through the morning sky
This elegant animal looks as though it
     should be queen of the birds
As it circles the marsh with the sun on
     its wings
Its long journey over
It falls from the sky, tumbling like a
     stone in a pond to the ground
It settles on the giant marsh with the
     other birds, wigeon, redshanks, Brent
     geese and Blackheaded gulls
The cold winter passed and the goose
     dissapeared into the sky ready to
     come again next year

by David, age 11

We felt that the children we teach should have a voice, and so the poem you have just read is the first of the poems by children which are included in the body of this chapter. Sometimes these poems have a direct relevance to a classroom account, sometimes not, but they are there for your delight and interest. In the interests of clarity, we have corrected some spelling and tidied up some punctuation, but in no other way have altered a word of the originals. We make no special claims for them, except that they are all from ordinary classes taught while the project was running and they are intended as a continual reminder of what we are about.

The first part of this chapter consists of accounts of the teaching of single poems by members of the project. These accounts are arranged in order of the age of the class, beginning with the younger children.

The second part of the chapter is arranged by poem rather than by age. We move from single poems to groups of related poems (Birds, Cats) taught by the same teacher, then to contrasting accounts of two poems ('Poem' and 'Follower') taught by several members of the group to their own classes in different schools. 'Poem' was chosen by the teachers themselves and is clearly a popular choice; it was used very effectively in primary and secondary schools. 'Follower,' on the other hand, was not chosen by the teachers themselves; they agreed to use it as a common starting-point, and it is interesting to note the difficulties that experienced teachers had in finding a successful 'way in' to a poem which they had not chosen.

We include the texts of the poems which are under discussion wherever appropriate. For the full sources of these poems, the reader is referred to Appendix A.

As teachers we are encouraged so much to value the autonomy or isolation of our own classrooms that it takes a great deal of courage to write any account of what we do for a wider public audience. So we offer these as samples of thoughtful, usually effective, but not always perfect, poetry teaching. We provide no easy 'ready-made' solutions and indeed perhaps provoke more questions than answers. Some of these will be found in our short 'Points to Ponder' sections, after each account. These attempt to draw your attention to and to pinpoint some of the issues being raised.

Some concerns are common to many of the individual accounts. There is very apparent agreement that the outcomes of the experience of poetry need not necessarily be written and that children can successfully come to terms with the language of poetry through the language of art and drama, for instance. There is agreement, too, about the need to follow up the experience of poetry through talk of all kinds, sometimes informal, sometimes carefully structured, part too of the art and the drama and an essential part of the process of children taking poetry to themselves.

Yet our poetry 'education' leads to some uneasiness. Concern about the place of the formal, as opposed to the informal, discussion of meaning begins to surface in one or two of our primary accounts. Those who feel that poetry is 'doing', and analysis inappropriate for the age/ability of the child, nonetheless feel that perhaps this is what they ought to be at. The clearly felt need to analyse is deeply embedded and apparent well before the demands of external examinations affect our ways of teaching in the secondary school.

But whatever our shortcomings and confusions, these accounts are authentic reflections of both the priorities and the personalities of practising and experienced teachers. They 'smell' of the classroom.

THE SHELL by James Stephens

And then I pressed the shell
Close to my ear,
And listened well.

And straightway, like a bell,
Came low and clear
The slow, sad, murmur of far distant seas

Whipped by an icy breeze
Upon a shore
Wind-swept and desolate.

It was a sunless strand that never bore
The footprint of a man,
Nor felt the weight

Since time began
Of any human quality or stir,
Save what the dreary winds and wave incur.

And in the hush of waters was the sound
Of pebbles, rolling round;
For ever rolling, with a hollow sound:

And bubbling sea-weeds, as the waters go,
Swish to and fro
Their long cold tentacles of slimy grey:

There was no day;
Nor ever came a night
Setting the stars alight

To wonder at the moon:
Was twilight only, and the frightened croon,
Smitten to whimpers, of the dreary wind

And waves that journeyed blind . . .
And then I loosed my ear — Oh, it was sweet
To hear a cart go jolting down the street.

Joan Varley

Mixed ability class of 9-10 year-olds

This poem fitted in very well with the Sea topic already being worked on in the classroom. I particularly wanted the children to use their imagination to think really hard about the pictures conjured up by the poem, and to decide why the poet thought of these things.

I wanted them to appreciate and be confronted by a descriptive poem, but one which they could also identify with; I felt that the sea, sand, shells, and islands were things which the children were fairly familiar with and could conjour up in their imaginations.

All the children had a copy of the poem which they read to themselves silently. They also had a rather beautiful shell which they seemed to enjoy holding to their ears as in the first lines of the poem. Then some children read parts of the poem aloud to us all. They picked words they liked, understood or did not understand. We used the record 'Jonathan Livingston Seagull' (sound-track to film) by Neil Diamond.[7] We listened to the music while we read the poem, worked and did art.

I planned that children should:

1. Discuss the meaning of the poem in a 'What do you think it meant?' article. This was to be written in the shape of a shell.

2. Write out the poem decoratively with illustrated borders.

3. Create a shell design with 'sea words' written amongst them.

4. Make circular 'porthole'-type pictures with greens/blues/white/yellow chalk swirls for a seascape, involving either a ship, a silhouette, a seagull or simply merging colours.

5. Make fish shapes with descriptive words (one on each fish) and hang shiny foil amongst an authentic fishing net with shells and glass floats.

The children enjoyed the challenge of discussing the feeling behind the poem; some entered into the discussion more readily, some found certain phrases difficult. In the main the written work was done enthusiastically and included intricate visual detail by many children. The art work evolved well and the children often asked for the music to be put on to work or draw to. They liked the fishing net strung across the windows and enjoyed the tiny glittering pieces of foil.

I was quite pleased because this was really the first time I had asked children to 'dissect' a poem. Their questioning and use of the imagination was quite good, really entering into the spirit of the far-away seas and shores, and they thought up lots of reasons why the poet thought of these things, e.g. had he once been shipwrecked and miraculously rescued? etc. To most of the class the poem conjured up a most beautiful place but to one child it was (in his own words) 'boring with nothing there, nothing happening'.

The children seemed to enjoy it and seemed absorbed making a booklet of the work. Boys particularly enjoyed it. I felt that good work came out of it.

The Sea

In the sea the sea was crashing against the rocks,
Bubbling Bubbling hot and cold in many places fish
    of many kinds,
Whales and sharks and other kinds of creatures
    great and small,
Seaweed that is like long tentacles slimy green and grey,
The sea is reflecting wavy foam, it is transparent,
And islands far above in the dull stormy wind.
The sea is green Blue and white dashing
Shells with tiny creatures in side are round about
Crabs are there too that nip your toes
I do not like the look of some creatures
    But I still like the sea

by Karen, age 10

Points to Ponder

(1) The contribution made by poetry to topic work.

(2) The value of reading poetry aloud:
i.e. the value of children trying the words for themselves and the enjoyment in saying poetry for the class as a whole.

(3) Writing: (i) re-creation of the original poem
(ii) extending the idea of the original poem
(iii) experimenting with shape.

(4) A sharing of ideas with other children and adults.

(5) The links with art work and perhaps with music.

FLANNAN ISLE by Wilfred Wilson Gibson

'Though three men dwell on Flannan Isle
To keep the lamp alight,
As we steered under the lee, we caught
No glimmer through the night.'

A passing ship at dawn had brought
The news, and quickly we set sail,
To find out what strange thing might ail
The keepers of the deep-sea light.

The winter day broke blue and bright
With glancing sun and glancing spray
While o'er the swell our boat made way,
As gallant as a gull in flight.

But as we neared the lonely Isle
And looked up at the naked height,
And saw the lighthouse towering white
With blinded lantern, that all night
Had never shot a spark
Of comfort through the dark,
So ghostly in the cold sunlight
It seemed that we were struck the while
With wonder all too dread for words.

And, as into the tiny creek
We stole beneath the hanging crag,
We saw three queer black ugly birds —
Too big by far in my belief,
For cormorant or shag —
Like seamen sitting bolt-upright
Up on a half-tide reef:
But, as we neared, they plunged from sight
Without a sound or spurt of white.

And still too mazed to speak,
We landed; and made fast the boat;
And climbed the track in single file,
Each wishing he was safe afloat
On any sea, however far,
So it be far from Flannan Isle:

And still we seemed to climb and climb
As though we'd lost all count of time
And so must climb for evermore.
Yet, all too soon, we reached the door —
The black, sun-blistered lighthouse-door,
That gaped for us ajar.

As, on the threshold, for a spell
We paused, we seemed to breathe the smell
Of limewash and of tar,
Familiar as our daily breath,
As though 'twere some strange scent of death;
And so yet wondering, side by side
We stood a moment still tongue-tied;
And each with black foreboding eyed
The door, ere we should fling it wide
To leave the sunlight for the gloom:
Till, plucking courage up, at last
Hard on each other's heels we passed
Into the living-room.

Yet, as we crowded through the door
We only saw a table, spread
For dinner, meat and cheese and bread;
But all untouched; and no one there:
As though, when they sat down to eat,
Ere they could even taste,
Alarm had come; and they in haste
Had risen and left the bread and meat,
For at the table-head a chair
Lay tumbled on the floor.

We listened, but we only heard
The feeble chirping of a bird
That starved upon its perch;
And, listening still, without a word
We set about our hopeless search.
We hunted high, we hunted low,
And soon ransacked the empty house;
Then o'er the Island, to and fro
We ranged, to listen and to look
In every cranny, cleft or nook
That might have hid a bird or mouse:

But though we searched from shore to shore
We found no sign in any place,
And soon again stood face to face
Before the gaping door,
And stole into the room once more
As frightened children steal.

Ay, though we hunted high and low
And hunted everywhere,
Of the three men's fate we found no trace
Of any kind in any place
But a door ajar, and an untouched meal,
And an overtoppled chair.

continued

And as we listened in the gloom
Of that forsaken living room —
A chill clutch on our breath —
We thought how ill-chance came to all
Who kept the Flannan Light,
And how the rock had been the death
Of many a likely lad —
How six had come to a sudden end
And three had gone stark mad,
And one whom we'd all known as a friend,
Had leapt from the lantern one still night,
And fallen dead by the lighthouse wall —
And long we thought
On the three we sought,
And on what might yet befall.

Like curs a glance has brought to heel
We listened, flinching there,
And looked, and looked, on the untouched meal,
And the overtoppled chair.

We seemed to stand for an endless while,
Though still no word was said,
Three men alive on Flannan Isle
Who thought on three men dead.

Joan Varley

Mixed ability class of 9-10 year-olds

This poem was chosen because it tells a story and is therefore a contrast to a descriptive poem (such as 'The Shell'). It is a mysterious story and lends itself to drama and movement with a lot of action. There are a great many possibilities with the open-ended outcome. All the class can be involved. Again, it linked with a Sea topic already underway.

I worked with the poem as follows:

1. I read it.
2. They read it in parts.
3. The whole class was then involved in some way by miming or acting it:
   — some were rocks
   — some the writhing sea — raising and lowering long strips of blue and green paper
   — the rowing sailors in the boat
   — the lighthouse
   — the birds.
4. Using a television studio setting, interviewing a survivor.
5. Writing a newspaper report — 'Strange things have been happening at the Flannan Isle Lighthouse . . . '
6. Giving a survivor's account.
7. Suggesting what happened next.

I hoped for the following outcomes:

(a) To create mystery; activity; drama.

(b) Lots of movement and miming activity with everyone taking part.
(c) Choral work.
(d) Discussion — because the outcome was left very much in the air.
(e) Reporting — eye-witness reports ('If I was there . . . ')

The responses of the children were very enthusiastic. The lurid details and the morbid and blood-curdling qualities of the poem appealed to them. The television approach was particularly good, with children being camera operators, outside broadcasters, interviewers. We had good crowd scenes with reporters jostling for stories.

A new ending/twist was invented. The children had some very clever suggestions. They invented a survivor who could talk about it, a corpse, and several other twists to the tale. The poem seemed to take over.

Some of the vocabulary of this poem was difficult, but the meaning came across, and the acting and the mime (which was very, very simple) made it vivid for those who at first did not understand.

The Lighthouse

I can see a lighthouse
From my bedroom window
at night I can see a ghost
Floating round the lighthouse

I hope you will not tell
that it is white and dangerous
here's a secret I can't tell
But I will tell it to you

Once I went upon the shore
and saw a ship at sea
then I saw a rowing boat
going up to the lighthouse

The sea was bashing and tossing over
the lighthouse stood bare
the light switched on like a torch
round and round it went

the man flung himself into the sea
I wonder why he did that
Well I'm glad that wasn't me

I went up to the lighthouse
to see what it could be
then I saw a ghost looking at me

continued

then I knew the lighthouse was haunted
the waves were big I left the door open
and the waves came crashing in
I ran upstairs and fell I was gone
but the lighthouse has been named the
mysterious lighthouse
and it stands to this very day

by Paula, age 10

Points to Ponder

(1) The value of an 'open-ended' story which makes possible all kinds of supposition about what might have happened.

(2) The way this is exploited in language work: television interviews with survivors, etc.

(3) Interviews and other talk which helps the children to make the poem their own so that they take it to themselves in a personal way and compare their experiences with the poem.

(4) The use of improvised mime/drama to establish the sequence of events.

BRAVE NEW WORLD by Spike Milligan

Twinkle Twinkle, little star
How I wonder what you are
Up above the sky so high
Like a diamond in the sky

Twinkle Twinkle, little star
I've just found out what you are
A lump of rusting rocket case
A rubbish tip in outer space.

Marylyn Grasar

Mixed ability class of 9-11 year-olds

For several lessons children looked at a variety of poetry books and chose their own favourite poem. Most children found it difficult to choose one 'favourite' among many.

I was amazed at the range of poems chosen and the reasons the children offered for their choice. When our class book of favourite poems was compiled, I picked one poem at random to duplicate and look at in more detail.

The child — Jason — who had chosen this poem did not wish to read it aloud himself, so I did. As we only had a half hour lesson, I wanted them to listen to Jason, to hear what had made him choose it, and then ask him questions. I also hoped that they might begin to look at the style of a particular poet, and look out for other poems of his in future reading.

Jason felt very important (this was one of my objectives); the rest were keen to ask questions and comment upon the poem. They noticed the use of nursery rhyme, and some suggested they might try this technique for themselves.

It was fortunate that this happened at a time when there was much publicity in the media about the space shuttle. There was general interest in space travel, and most children seemed fairly knowledgeable about it. I think it increased their interest in this particular poem to know something of Spike Milligan, whom they have seen on television.

This was the first time I had tried this method with this class, and I was quite pleased with their reaction. Had the lesson been longer, I would have had more Milligan poems available for them to look at. I have a Milligan anthology of my own, which I leave in the class, and most of the children have looked at it voluntarily. The brevity and wit of his poems appeal to them.

The Face

I see a face
Up in space
What can it be?
Don't ask me

Stars shining bright
It gives me a fright
But what can it be
That face in space?

Moon so light
Such a beautiful sight
But what is that face
Up in space?

by Jane, age 11

Points to Ponder

(1) The sharing of one child's enthusiasm for a particular poem with other children.

(2) The beginnings of an awareness of different poetic techniques.

(3) The appeal of a particular poet.

MY MOTHER SAW A DANCING BEAR by Charles Causley

My mother saw a dancing bear
By the schoolyard, a day in June.
The keeper stood with chain and bar
And whistle-pipe, and played a tune.

And bruin lifted up its head
And lifted up its dusty feet,
And all the children laughed to see
It caper in the summer heat.

They watched as for the Queen it died.
They watched it march. They watched it halt.
They heard the keeper as he cried,
'Now, roly-poly!' 'Somersault!'

And then, my mother said, there came
The keeper with a begging-cup,
The bear with burning coat of fur,
Shaming the laughter to a stop.

They paid a penny for the dance,
But what they saw was not the show;
Only, in bruin's aching eyes,
Far-distant forests, and the snow.

Eveline Fullwood

Mixed ability class of 9-11 year-olds

I chose this poem because it is a great favourite of mine, and however many times I either hear or read it I am always moved by it. I wanted to find out what depth of feeling the children might experience through it. I also wanted to use it in the 'Poetry for Pleasure' afternoon (see Chapter III, p. 57) that I had planned, in order to introduce a different mood — most of the other poems chosen being light-hearted.

The children had their own copy of the words which I read to them once. I asked the children to think particularly about the bear whilst I read the poem a second time. The children were very enthusiastic about the poem — 'even though it's sad', and we had a most worthwhile discussion about what the feelings of the bear must have been, and what kind of man the keeper was — cruel or kind?

This led on to a discussion about cruelty to animals and also about the changes that have taken place in entertainment over the years. The annual visit of the fair to the village is one of the highlights of the children's year, and so we talked about the early travelling fairs and entertainers and how the performing animals, the jugglers and acrobats now travel round together with the circus rather than alone as they did in earlier times.

My children, being 'doers', then came up with the request — 'Can we act it?' This we did, the children deciding how it could be done and suggesting and providing the costumes. They used the reference library to find the type of clothes worn in the period, and became very engrossed in the information they found about travelling entertainers.

They also did the casting, and once again showed how very good they are at choosing the right people — though sometimes a little unobtrusive guidance is needed! However, one of the most disruptive boys in the class became a superb dancing bear, and one of the girls taught the keeper to play his 'tune' on a recorder.

Background music was the next requirement, and I chose two pieces of music that I thought might be suitable:

(i)   Saint-Saens, Carnival of the Animals — 'Elephants and Tortoises'.
(ii) Greig, Peer Gynt Suite — 'Solveig's Song'.

After listening carefully to these two pieces the children chose Solveig's Song because they thought that it was 'slow and heavy enough' and also 'sad enough' to fit the poem.

I now wanted them to produce some work of their own — how much of the 'feeling' in the poem had the children absorbed? Only two children from the class of thirty elected to write a story instead of a poem, and the poems that were written showed that I had, in part, achieved what I set out to do — the feeling had transferred itself to the children and was shown in their own poems. For some children drama is a more easy means of expression than writing, and for some in the class, particularly the bear, acting out was an opportunity to express feeling. The children illustrated their poems and wrote them out in their own poetry books.

Finally, a large class picture was produced to which every child contributed at least one person for the crowd.

I felt that the teaching of the poem had been successful because of:

(a)   the children's obvious pleasure in it — and surely this is the main aim in teaching poetry,

(b)   the speed with which it was voluntarily learnt,

(c)   the poems which they produced themselves.

This is a difficult poem and all the poetry work of the past year was an experience on which to draw when writing about the bear.

Take Me Back

Oh please God make my wish come true
I hate the tricks that I have to do
I long to be at home with the trees
The grass, the flowers and the leaves

I want to roam there once again
But here I am at the end of my chain
Dancing for the people's pleasure
I'd much rather lumber in the heather

I'd love to run away one day
But how would I ever find my way
To the place where I once ran free
It seems so far away to me

I like my keeper, he's quite kind
But the place I had to leave behind
Was much more lovelier than here
But I'll never see it again I fear

I suppose I'll have to put up with this
Instead of having the life I miss
I know that it's hopeless when I say
I'll see my land again one day.

by Rachel, age 10

Points to Ponder

(1) A poem of complex feelings and emotions — chosen to extend the poetic experience of this class.

(2) A more formal use of drama — costumes researched in the reference library.

(3) The realization that, for some, 'drama is a more easy form of expression than writing'.

(4) Learning by heart need not be a chore and can be voluntary!

(5) The value of previous work on poetry on which the class is able to draw.

MY DAD'S THUMB by Michael Rosen

My dad's thumb
can stick pins in wood
without flinching —
it can crush family-size matchboxes
in one stroke
and lever off jam-jar lids without piercing
at the pierce here sign.

If it wanted
it could be a bath-plug
or a paint-scraper
a keyhole cover or a tap-tightener.

It's already a great nutcracker
and if it dressed up
it could easily pass
as a broad bean or a big toe.

In actual fact, it's quite simply
the world's fastest envelope burster.

Edith Chambers

Mixed ability class of 10-11 year-olds

I had taken a morning assembly on the use of our hands and how we should feel if we had none. I then pursued this in the classroom, having reminded the children of how we tried to perceive clearly with 'the poet's eye' and express what we saw or felt in words. I asked them to think of somebody's hands, which they had watched, doing perhaps skilled work or ordinary everyday things. I told them my own experience of watching my mother, who was a baker by trade, creaming sugar and margarine with her hand and rolling two loaves at the same time, one in each hand. I then read to them Michael Rosen's poem and also a prose extract from a biography of Maria Callas: 'Just to watch Miss Callas' hands at work almost recreated the opera. They caressed, stretched out in love and hatred, fluttered helplessly like a caged bird . . . At times she even sang through her hands.'[8] We had a short talk about an actor's hands and then the children wrote a poem with the title 'Hands'.

There was readiness on the part of most of the children to tell me what they had noticed which they liked or disliked. One boy liked to see his mother going round her lips with a little finger after she had put lipstick on. Some of the girls spoke of watching their mother doing everyday household jobs — dusting, washing. One girl loved her dad's hand when it blew her a kiss. Most of them loved to feel Mum's hands when they were ill, and they had to be washed, or just comforted. Another boy said his mother's hands 'looked like an old age person' because she washed up every night at a public house.

The poems produced were what I wanted — their own 'poet's eye'.

Hands

Hands are very fast at their work
Hands can write hands can type
Hands have fingers which twiddle and bend
Hands can be double jointed
My hand can catch and scratch
Hands! Hands! Hands!
There's things to do, things to play
And many more things you can do with your hands
Hands are very good at baking
Raking and making things
PICKPOCKETS they use their hands
For stealing and thieving
You can use your hands for sewing and weaving
Your hands can be used
For handstands and goalkeeping
In Netball girls use their hands
For throwing and catching
In plays they use their hands
To describe what they're doing
People who cannot hear
Use their hands for sign language
There are many more things to do with your hands.

by Dale, age 11

Points to Ponder

(1) The value of wide reading to the teacher.

(2) The value of individual personal experience and of children's very detailed observation.

WHAT HAS HAPPENED TO LULU? by Charles Causley

What has happened to Lulu, mother?
  What has happened to Lu?
There's nothing in her bed but an old rag-doll
  And by its side a shoe.

Why is her window wide, mother,
  The curtain flapping free,
And only a circle on the dusty shelf
  Where her money-box used to be?

Why do you turn your head, mother,
  And why do the tear-drops fall?
And why do you crumple that note on the fire
  And say it is nothing at all?

I woke to voices late last night,
  I heard an engine roar.
Why do you tell me the things I heard
  Were a dream and nothing more?

I heard somebody cry, mother,
  In anger or in pain,
But now I ask you why, mother,
  You say it was a gust of rain.

Why do you wander about as though
  You don't know what to do?
What has happened to Lulu, mother?
  What has happened to Lu?

Joan Barker

Mixed ability class of 10-11 year-olds

The focus of attention in the poetry corner had been Charles Causley with posters of his poems displayed together with anthologies of his poetry. 'What has happened to Lulu?' was just one in a series of his poems read to the class during two weeks.

I read the poem to the class once, and then I asked them to think about what might have happened whilst I read it a second time. We had a discussion about the possible events of the night, leading up to strip-cartoon drawings to tell the whole story. The children joined in the discussion enthusiastically and had lots of different ideas about what had happened. Quite a lot of time was spent deciding how old Lulu had been as this could have a bearing on why she had gone. Also there were conflicting opinions on the note — was it from Lulu? Or was it a ransom demand note? They spent a great deal of time and effort planning and executing their cartoon drawings either as a complete page or a book with one picture on each page.

I felt that their responses had been favourable towards the poem judging by the quality of their finished work. They obviously enjoyed it, and it has since been added to the class anthology of favourite poems.

As my aim had been to provide the children with an enjoyable experience and to familiarize them with a particular poet's work, I felt that it had been a successful venture. Because they had had to refer to the poem to produce their work, this had ensured familiarity with the text without it being laboured.

The Deserted House

There's no Smoke in the chimney
And the rain comes in the hall
There's no glass in the window
And no door in the wall.

No-one had tended the garden
The walls are grey and bare
The traffic on the road passes by
But no-one enters there
But the memories of the house live on
With the ghosts who linger there.

by Jane, age 10

Points to Ponder

(1) Concentration upon the work of one particular poet.

(2) The use of strip-cartoon drawings to explore the meaning of the poem.

(3) Again the value of an open-ended story, particularly for language work.

A CASE OF MURDER by Vernon Scannell

They should not have left him there alone,
Alone that is except for the cat.
He was only nine, not old enough
To be left alone in a basement flat,
Alone, that is, except for the cat.
A dog would have been a different thing,
A big gruff dog with slashing jaws,
But a cat with round eyes mad as gold,
Plump as a cushion with tucked-in paws—
Better have left him with a fair-sized rat!
But what they did was leave him with a cat.
He hated that cat; he watched it sit,
A buzzing machine of soft black stuff,
He sat and watched and he hated it,
Snug in its fur, hot blood in a muff,
And its mad gold stare and the way it sat
Crooning dark warmth: he loathed all that.
So he took Daddy's stick and he hit the cat.
Then quick as a sudden crack in glass
It hissed, black flash, to a hiding place
In the dust and dark beneath the couch,
And he followed the grin on his new-made face,
A wide-eyed, frightened snarl of a grin,
And he took the stick and he thrust it in,
Hard and quick in the furry dark.

The black fur squealed and he felt his skin
Prickle with sparks of dry delight.
Then the cat again came into sight,
Shot for the door that wasn't quite shut,
But the boy, quick too, slammed fast the door:
The cat, half-through, was cracked like a nut
And the soft black thud was dumped on the floor.
Then the boy was suddenly terrified
And he bit his knuckles and cried and cried;
But he had to do something with the dead thing there.
His eyes squeezed beads of salty prayer
But the wound of fear gaped wide and raw;
He dared not touch the thing with his hands
So he fetched a spade and shovelled it
And dumped the load of heavy fur.
In the spidery cupboard under the stair
Where it's been for years, and though it died
It's grown in that cupboard and its hot low purr
Grows slowly louder year by year:
There'll not be a corner for the boy to hide
When the cupboard swells and all sides split
And the huge black cat pads out of it.

David Bennett

Mixed ability class of 11-12 year-olds

A 'talks' lesson led some pupils to talk about their pets, which eventually led into animals and cruelty to animals. Here I stopped discussion, deferred it to another lesson, and prepared to read them the poem as my contribution to their discussion.

In the following lesson, I reminded them of the earlier lesson, and invited their anecdotes about animals. When we got to discussing cruelty I asked how many had witnessed cruelty to animals. After several contributions I announced that I had read something which I wanted to share with them and said that I would be interested in their response.

I read it once. They read it to themselves, and then they worked in pairs on the following questions, which I had previously written on the back of the board.

(a)   What questions arise in your mind from the poem?

(b)   Who is to blame for what happened?

(c)   Where might Scannell have found the idea?

(d)   How do you feel about it? Should such things be written about?

I wanted them to explore the poem through the structured questions in order to:

(i)   find personal value in the poem

(ii)   establish a constructive 'talk' situation.

Predictably, the children found the poem violent. They found the ending confusing, but realized its real meaning once a classmate had pointed this out. Few of them asked questions about the vocabulary or imagery. They had firm ideas on who was to blame, fanciful ideas on the original structure and ambivalent attitudes towards the violence.

For homework the children were asked to write the conversation in the household when the parents came home. (They had recently done work on speech punctuation.) They were told that a page of speech would be sufficient. Few did less than two pages and whilst the speech punctuation was often poor, the content of the conversations were some of the best they have produced.

Unfortunately this came just at Christmas time when school life becomes frayed. I would have liked to go on to writing and collecting animal poems — especially about cats and perhaps feelings against cats. A closer look at the language and structure of the poem would be another priority in future.

Swords & Ploughshares

Swords are the killers at war.
Withering bodies fall down before the swords.
Over the countryside the ground is strewn with bodies.
Red is the colour of the grass
Death was the final victor.
Silence reigned in the battle fields once more.

Ploughing fields in the dry hot sun,
Lowering the shares into the ground,
Out of the earth come sun-ripened crops.
Under the soil seeds struggled for life.
Growing was very hard for them.
Holes were made to plant fresh seeds,
Sowing them quickly to race against time,
Having failed the first crop.
A small green shoot shows above the ground.
Rain finally comes to save the thirsty land.
Each little plant welcomes every drop.
Soon they are full grown to feed hungry mouths.

by David, age 11

Points to Ponder

(1) The teacher's concern that the children should find personal value in the poem.

(2) The use of structured questions to establish a constructive talk situation.

(3) The need to begin to take more account of the language and structure of the poem itself.

JABBERWOCKY by Lewis Carroll

'Twas brillig, and the slithy toves
 Did gyre and gimble in the wabe;
All momsy were the borogoves,
 And the mome raths outgrabe.

'Beware the Jabberwock, my son!
 The jaws that bite, the claws that catch!
Beware the Jubjub bird, and shun
 The frumious Bandersnatch!'

He took his vorpal sword in hand:
 Long time the manxome foe he sought —
So rested he by the Tumtum tree,
 And stood awhile in thought.

And as in uffish thought he stood,
 The Jabberwock, with eyes of flame,
Came whiffling through the tulgey wood,
 And burbled as it came!

One, two! One, two! And through and through
 The vorpal blade went snicker-snack!
He left it dead, and with its head
 He went galumphing back.

'And hast thou slain the Jabberwock?
 Come to my arms, my beamish boy!
O frabjous day! Callooh! Callay!
 He chortled in his joy.

'Twas brillig, and the slithy toves
 Did gyre and gimble in the wabe;
All mimsy were the borogoves,
 And the mome raths outgrabe.

David Bennett

Lower band ability class of 12-13 year-olds

(1) I simply announced that I was going to read them a poem that I couldn't fully understand and did so, twice, very dramatically.

(2) The intrigue that was aroused in this otherwise 'stodgy' class was immediately apparent. A tremendous flow of creative ideas was generated as they speculated upon its characters and meanings.

(3) Being a class that draws better than it writes, they were soon embarking upon elaborate portraits of Jubjubs, Slithy Toves and all else, mainly in fluorescent felt-tip!

(4) To round off that particular lesson we read the whole duplicated poem together in dramatic and frayed unison.

(5) The next lesson we looked at the poem again, this time thinking about what might have happened before and after, and then, following a revision of a newspaper layout, we combined the pictures and our discussion into front pages:
     'Manxome Foe Destroyed'
     'Jabberwocky Slain at Last'
     'Strange Affair in Tulgeywood'
     'Victory for Beamish Boy'
     'Fruminous Creature spotted in Toton'

(6) Building upon this I did the same work with a middle band, first-year class, but began differently. This time I wrote some of the more bizarre words on the board and asked children to jot down what they thought they meant. The poem followed our discussion, and we attempted to discover whether the pupils' meanings might make some sense of the poem.

(7) The drawing and news reporting followed.

(8) We then returned to the poem and examined its rhythm and rhyme together, looking for patterns that could be emulated. (They had recently done some syllable-counting in music, which helped.) Then they were asked to re-write the first two verses, more if they wished, substituting their own bizarre words and keeping to the original rhythm and rhyme pattern. These were marked by their classmates, then by me.

(9) Eventually the whole set of work was assembled for an Open Evening display.

It was during the syllable-counting session that I overheard a trio of girls discussing how much more interesting English was at secondary school than at their junior schools (they had attended different feeder schools). Hence I now have a warm regard for 'Jabberwocky'. Seriously, I feel that its imaginative power is inspiring and exciting to even the most reluctant pupils. Little wonder it has given rise to other, professional, artistic enterprises. The drama possibilities and opportunities for choral speaking exercises would definitely be worth exploring on a future occasion as an extension to the imaginative response.

Many children were pleasantly bewildered by the re-working exercise, especially the poor spellers, since their version of words couldn't possibly be wrong. After a while the bewilderment edged into a liberation, which, as an afterthought, I might have capitalized upon. I could have looked at, or at least introduced, more poems with zany words — Spike Milligan's verse for example, afterwards encouraging the writing of nonsense verse by the pupils, which would probably come off best on tape.

Jabberwocky

'Twas sloopy and the
Blontig dings
Did loove and bingle
In the grob.
All dothywere the
Wanderlings
And punt lops venlop.

Beware the puggerby
my tod
The Lars that buck,
the dicks that litch.
Beware the boo-boo bud
The venduious loggy
titch.

by Carolyn, age 11

Points to Ponder

(1) The use of art work to focus upon the language of the poem.

MY PARTY by Kit Wright

My parents said I could have a party
And that's just what I did.

Dad said, "Who had you thought of inviting?"
I told him. He said, "Well, you'd better start writing,"
And that's just what I did

To:
Phyllis Willis, Horace Morris,
Nancy, Clancy, Bert and Gert Sturt,
Dick and Mick and Nick Crick,
Ron, Don, John,
Dolly, Molly, Polly—
Neil Peel—
And my dear old friend, Dave Dirt.

I wrote, "Come along, I'm having a party,"
And that's just what they did.

They all arrived with huge appetites
As Dad and I were fixing the lights.
I said, "Help yourself to the drinks and bites!"
And that's just what they did,
All of them:

Phyllis Willis, Horace Morris,
Nancy, Clancy, Bert and Gert Sturt,
Dick and Mick and Nick Crick,
Ron, Don, John,
Dolly, Molly, Polly—
Neil Peel—
And my dear old friend, Dave Dirt.

Now, I had a good time and as far as I could tell,
The party seemed to go pretty well—
Yes, that's just what it did.

Then Dad said, "Come on, just for fun,
Let's have a *turn* from everyone!"
And a turn's just what they did,

All of them:

Phyllis Willis, Horace Morris,
Nancy, Clancy, Bert and Gert Sturt,
Dick and Mick and Nick Crick,
Ron, Don, John,
Dolly, Molly, Polly—
Neil Peel—
And my dear old friend, Dave Dirt.

AND THIS IS WHAT THEY DID:

Phyllis and Clancy
And Horace and Nancy
Did a song and dance number
That was really fancy—

Dolly, Molly, Polly,
Ron, Don and John
Performed a play
That went on and on and on—

Gert and Bert Sturt,
Sister and brother,
Did an imitation of
Each other.

(Gert Sturt put on Bert Sturt's shirt
And Bert Sturt put on Gert Sturt's skirt.)

Neil Peel
All on his own
Danced an eightsome reel.

Dick and Mick
And Nicholas Crick
Did a most *ingenious*
Conjuring trick

And my dear old friend, Dave Dirt,
Was terribly sick
All over the flowers.
We cleaned it up.
It took *hours*.

But as Dad said, giving a party's not easy.
You really
Have to
Stick at it.
I agree. And if Dave gives a party
I'm certainly
Going to be
Sick at it.

Jackie Severn

Mixed ability class of 12-13 year-olds

I was introduced to this poem during a poetry course. Some other teachers and I chose it from several offered to us to produce and present, using movement and simple instruments. I had found it both lively and amusing, and felt that the subject-matter of the poem was eminently suitable for this particular class, most of the pupils being naturally quite lively and fun-loving. Also, it seemed a reasonable topic to catch the interest of this age group, and presenting it was an ideal opportunity to involve every member of the class in an activity.

Initially, I simply read the poem to the children, having steeled myself to 'play the fool' in order to make my reading of the poem come alive. I explained to the children how I had met the poem, and how a dozen or so teachers on the course had made complete and utter fools of themselves performing to fellow teachers, advisers, and so on, and thoroughly enjoyed it. This information seemed to ignite a certain spark of imagination in even the least poetic amongst the class!

I had two main purposes in using the poem:

(a) to coerce the whole class into working together on a choral presentation of the poem, directed by me, with a possible view to tape-recording, and

(b) to divide the class into two groups, each to 'present' the poem to the rest of us, in whatever form they wished, using any methods, means, or materials they wished.

The whole class appreciated my initial reading of the poem (accents, sound effects, gestures and all!) and confirmed my belief that it really is worth making a spectacle of yourself at times! They laughed in all the right places during the initial hearing, and made appropriate noises and gestures of revulsion and shock during the places where people were being sick. On questioning, they all said that they liked the poem, for various reasons: because it was different; amusing; reminded them of being sick at a party, and so on.

They were very enthusiastic about producing the poem as a choral piece, especially if it was to be recorded, and became extremely cross with each other when errors occurred! They were all brimming with ideas about how to present it, using drama and sound effects, and, although the organization of the two groups varied enormously, they all seemed to enjoy 'doing their bit'.

I was pleased with the children's responses, which I evaluated in several different ways:

(a) Talking to the class, as a whole, initially, after the first reading by myself;

(b) Observing the ways in which the two groups organized themselves, and distributed the work-load of the presentation, e.g. 'I've only got one line; can't I say more?'; and all of the boys wanted to be Dave Dirt!

(c) Asking another English teacher (the group tutor of quite a few of the children in the class) to come to watch the final presentations; and then listening to her opinions afterwards, her initial reaction being, 'Can I borrow your class set of the poem?'

(d)   Listening to the children's ad-lib. comments after the presentations, e.g. 'We could have . . .'; 'I wish we'd . . .'.

I learned a lot from the splitting of this class into two groups. The division was random, group one consisted of the first 6 boys on my register and the first 8 girls; group two being the other 7 boys and 8 girls. Since the class was of mixed ability, I foresaw no problems, but found that many of the brighter pupils happened to be in the same group. In my opinion, however, the noisier, what could be called 'less able' group produced the best presentation by far, with props, noises etc., whereas the other group sat in a circle and simply read its lines.

I felt that the whole activity had been worthwhile and quite illuminating. A new bond had been created between this particular class and myself, due to the fact that we had all made fools of ourselves in some way and lost some of our inhibitions with each other (except that they now want me to read poems to them 'just like you did the other one, Miss'). I think it's at least one poem that the children will remember, because they each took an active part in their own presentation.

Merry

Jolly Sherry
Very merry
Sparkling Perry
Uncle Jerry
Have some
Sherry,
And let's be
MERRY

by Martin, age 11

Points to Ponder

(1)   The use made of a choral presentation of the poem.

(2)   The use made of a 'formal' presentation with props, sound effects etc.

(3)   The way in which the experience of the poem drew the class and the teacher closer together.

HARD CHEESE by Justin St John

The grown-ups are all safe,
Tucked up inside,
Where they belong.

They doze into the telly,
Bustle through the washing-up,
Snore into the fire,
Rustle through the paper.

They're all there,
Out of harm's way.

Now it's *our* street:
All the back-yards,
All the gardens,
All the shadows,
All the dark corners,
All the privet-hedges,
All the lamp-posts,
All the door-ways.

Here is an important announcement:
The army of occupation
Is confined to barracks.
Hooray.

We're the natives.
We creep out at night,
Play everywhere,
Swing on *all* the lamp-posts,
Slit your gizzard?

Then, about nine o'clock,
They send out search-parties.

We can hear them coming.
And we crouch
In the garden-sheds,
Behind the dust-bins,

Up the alley-ways,
Inside the dust-bins,
Or stand stock-still,
And pull ourselves in,
As thin as a pin,
Behind the lamp-posts.

And they stand still,
And peer into the dark.
They take a deep breath —
You can hear it for miles —
And, then, they bawl,
They shout, they caterwaul:
'J-i-i-i-i-i-mmeeee!'
'Timeforbed. D'youhearme?'
'M-a-a-a-a-a-reeee!'
'J-o-o-o-o-o-hnneeee!'
'S-a-a-a-a-a-mmeeee!'
'Mary!' 'Jimmy!'
'Johnny!' 'Sammy!'
Like cats. With very big mouths.

Then we give ourselves up,
Prisoners — of — war.
Till tomorrow night.

But just you wait.
One of these nights
We'll hold out,
We'll lie doggo,
And wait, and wait,
Till they just give up
And mumble
And go to bed.
You just wait.
They'll see!

Lynn Wood

Mixed ability class of 10-11 year-olds

I felt that the children would be able to relate well to this poem as it presents a situation in which they often find themselves, living on a big estate. It's a poem I like and I thought the class would enjoy and appreciate it. We began with a discussion about how the children occupy themselves outside after school and this led up to a reading of the poem. All the children had their own copy of the poem which they read on their own first, then I read the poem aloud to the class.

I wanted to have a day of fun where the whole class worked together on the same thing. I hoped that they would produce a frieze together. This would tell the story in picture form and include a sentence from the poem chosen to illustrate each picture. We also made a folder of written work which included various explanations of the games children played, together with the children's own pictures of them. I also wanted them to act out the poem together, partly for enjoyment and perhaps at a later date to use the poem as the basis for a class assembly. So we did some drama — stealthy movements, hiding, noisy/quiet movements, control of movement, i.e. acting out the reality of their own lives.

The children were delighted with the poem and worked with enthusiasm. I think the session was successful as the children worked happily together and were pleased with the results of their work.

What is it?

What is it?
It's a dark blanket
coming down on every body.

What is it?
It's a big black cloud
coming over

What is it?
It's like the Sun
dropping out of the Sky

What is it?
It's the dark
cold night.

by Mark, age 11

Points to Ponder

(1) A whole day of 'fun' based upon a poem.

POSTING LETTERS by Gregory Harrison

There are no lamps in our village,
And when the owl-and-bat black night
Creeps up low fields
And sidles along the manor walls
I walk quickly.

It is winter;
The letters patter from my hand
Into the tin box in the cottage wall;
The gate taps behind me,
And the road in the sliver of moonlight
Gleams greasily
Where the tractors have stood.

I have to go under the spread fingers of the trees
Under the dark windows of the old man's house,
Where the panes in peeling frames
Flash like spectacles
As I tip-toe.
But there is no sound of him in his one room
In the Queen-Anne shell,
Behind the shutters.

I run past the gates,
Their iron feet gaitered with grass,
Into the church porch,
Perhaps for sanctuary,
Standing, hand on the cold door ring,
While above
The tongue-tip of the clock
Clops
Against the hard palate of the tower.

The door groans as I push
And
Dare myself to dash
Along the flagstones to the great brass bird,
To put one shrinking hand
Upon the gritty lid
Of Black Tom's tomb.

Don't tempt whatever spirits stir
In this damp corner,
But
Race down the aisle,
Blunder past font,
Fumble the door,
Leap steps,
Clang iron gate,
And patter through the short-cut muddy lane.

Oh, what a pumping of breath
And choking throat
For three letters.
And now there are the cattle
Stirring in the straw
So close
I can hear their soft muzzling and coughs;
And there are the bungalows,
And the steel-blue miming of the little screen;
And the familiar rattle of the latch
And our own knocker
Clicking like an old friend;
And
I am home.

<u>Joan Barker</u>

Mixed ability class of 10-11 year-olds

I combined 'Posting Letters' with 'Hard Cheese' (see p. 27). The two poems showed different aspects of being out at night — one enjoyable and one not. Most of the children would have experienced both situations and could, therefore, compare them and personally respond to the poems.

I read 'Hard Cheese' to the class (they had copies of all the poems). We talked about the things we would do if we could stay out all night. Having savoured the enjoyment of this situation I then read 'Midnight Wood',[9] to create an entirely different atmosphere. Without any further discussion I read 'Posting Letters' which was followed by a lengthy discussion about what we were afraid of. I ended by reading 'Who's That?'[10]

Following the readings of the poems I wanted the class to prepare one of the poems to present to the rest of the class. They worked in small groups. I then wanted to see how much of the poem the children could recall the following day. I decided to let them work in pairs writing as much of the poem as they could remember.

The children entered freely into both discussions, deciding that it was being on your own that made the dark frightening — even the cat helped! Many other fears were talked about as well as plenty of anecdotes about enjoying the dark with friends. The class divided up into four groups of varying sizes and worked enthusiastically on their presentations. All four groups chose to do 'Hard Cheese,' but in quite different ways, although all were based on choral speaking and drama. Afterwards they were all quite eager to talk about how they could be improved.

In response to the suggestion that they tried to write out the poem, discussing it with a partner, they worked very hard, many of them going off on their own after the first few lines to produce an almost completely correct version of a very long poem.

They then formed other groups to present one of the other poems in a different way — voices and sound effects, musical instruments, etc. I felt that the teaching of the poems was successful, since although the discussions and the presentations might seem to be the main point of the venture, we didn't at any time lose sight of the poems themselves and constant reference was made to them in both activities.

The children obviously got a great deal of enjoyment out of their work as they worked on through playtime and lunchtime without really noticing.

Night

The night is drawing near
And with it comes the fear
Of ghosts and spooks and horrid things
The fear that only nightime brings.

A distant noise
A hazy light
Can always bring the
Fear of night.

The night is black
The air is cold
The wind blows strong
The fear unfolds.

It may be the sound
Of a wolf on the prowl
That makes you afraid with its
Terrible howl.

by Paul, age 11

Points to Ponder

(1)   Again the use of a 'formal' presentation involving choral speaking, drama, voices, sound effects, musical instruments.

'THE EAGLE', 'THE GREAT GULLS' and 'HAWK ROOSTING'

THE EAGLE by Alfred Lord Tennyson

He clasps the crag with crooked hands;
Close to the sun in lonely lands,
Ring'd with the azure world, he stands.

The wrinkled sea beneath him crawls;
He watches from his mountain walls,
And like a thunderbolt he falls.

THE GREAT GULLS by Andrew Penwarden (aged 10)

Screaming and shrieking,
Yelling and crying,
Leaping and diving
Above a sea boiling and writhing
Crashing and smashing,
Their black backs shining,
And plunging down screaming
On to a sea bulging and foaming
Slushing and roaring—
A cauldron of movement.

HAWK ROOSTING by Ted Hughes

I sit in the top of the wood, my eyes closed.
Inaction, no falsifying dream
Between my hooked head and hooked feet:
Or in sleep rehearse perfect kills and eat.

The convenience of the high trees!
The air's buoyancy and the sun's ray
Are of advantage to me;
And the earth's face upward for my inspection.

My feet are locked upon the rough bark.
It took the whole of Creation
To produce my foot, my each feather:
Now I hold Creation in my foot

Or fly up, and revolve it all slowly—
I kill where I please because it is all mine.
There is no sophistry in my body:
My manners are tearing off heads—

The allotment of death.
For the one path of my flight is direct
Through the bones of the living.
No arguments assert my right:

The sun is behind me.
Nothing has changed since I began.
My eye has permitted no change.
I am going to keep things like this.

David Bennett

Middle band ability class of 11-12 year-olds

This work was begun as a hasty precursor to a poetry competition being organized as part of a House Arts Festival. Pupils were asked to write a poem on the subject of 'a bird' or 'birds'.

The first two poems were duplicated, minus their titles, and presented to the pupils. They were given five minutes to read them and cogitate over them in silence with two questions to answer — what was being written about? How do you know? A discussion and exchange of ideas followed, one poem at a time; broad ideas were noted on the board followed by a vote for the most feasible suggestion. (This was a useful way to stimulate interest and profitable discussion, probably better done in groups in future.) Then children were told the titles and asked whether there was anything about the poem that they still wanted to know. With skilful manipulation the class usually answers its own questions and learns a lot more in the process.

I summarized what had gone before and talked about the special qualities that distinguish one bird from another, e.g. the 'hawkishness of hawks', the 'seagullness of seagulls', the 'owlishness of owls' etc. We went back to the poems and recapped on the words and phrases that were relevant there. Then the class began their own bird poems, using pictures from library books to help them. These were completed for homework and then copied out as competition entries.

In far less pressing circumstances I would like to do more with this, trying to evoke more enthusiasm, thought and knowledge by having groups look at pictures and slides or stuffed specimens. An accompanying anthology of bird poems, collected and illustrated by the pupils would also be a valuable exercise. The concepts that I tried to get across in a short while needed longer to be absorbed before the final exercise was begun.

After this experience I worked with a bottom band ability, second year class on the same project, similarly pressed for time. I began by dividing the blackboard in half and invited their ideas on what made an owl an owl and a robin a robin. All the various possibilities were written up and then the two poems were looked at briefly and discussed in the light of the previous exercise. The pupils' own poems followed, mainly using ideas from the board. This was completed for homework, some choosing to use the acrostic form, which many lower ability pupils find a very secure form with which to work (see T. Webster's discussion of this on page 80).

With a fourth year O-level group I initially used the first two and a half verses of Ted Hughes' poem, minus the title, previously written on the board. I followed that up with an examination of the whole poem based upon the pupils' own questions about it, which they had arrived at after fifteen minutes discussion of the poem in pairs. Most found it very difficult but all except two pupils agreed that it had been a very rewarding poem to study. Certainly the deep thinking that it provoked was reflected in their final writing.

The Kestrel

This sly bird
        swoops
            dives
        to catch his prey
            his
                brown
                    head
                motionless
            pointing
        beak.
        long
    swift
  wings
clawing his prey

Then, an occupied silence

by Julie, age 11

Points to Ponder

(1) Language work — trying to capture the essence of each bird in words and looking back to the poems for language that is relevant.

(2) Then comparing this language with the 'real' thing.

'CATS'

A Group of Cat Poems

CAT! by Eleanor Farjeon

> *Cat!*
> Scat!
> Atter her, atter her,
> Sleeky flatterer,
> Spitfire chatterer,
> Scatter her, scatter her
>   Off her mat!
>   *Wuff!*
>   *Wuff!*
>   Treat her rough!
> Git her, git her,
> Whiskery spitter!
> Catch her, catch her,
> Green-eyed scratcher!
>   Slathery
>   Slithery
>   Hisser,
>   Don't miss her!
> Run till you're dithery,
>   Hithery
>   Thithery
>   *Pfitts! pfitts!*
>   How she spits!
>   *Spitch! Spatch!*
>   Can't she scratch!
> Scritching the bark
> Of the sycamore-tree,
> She's reached her ark
> And's hissing at me
>   *Pfitts! pfitts!*
>   *Wuff! wuff!*
>   Scat,
>   Cat!
>   That's
>   *That!*

MISS TIBBLES by Ian Serraillier

> Miss Tibbles is my kitten; white
> As day she is and black as night.
>
> She moves in little gusts and breezes
> Sharp and sudden as a sneeze is.
>
> At hunting Tibbles has no match.
> How I like to see her catch
>
> Moth or beetle, two a penny,
> And feast until there isn't any!
>
> Or, if they 'scape her, see her eyes
> Grow big as saucers with surprise.
>
> Sometimes I like her calm, unwild,
> Gentle as a sleeping child,
>
> And wonder as she lies, a fur ring,
> Curled upon my lap, unstirring,
> Is it me or Tibbles purring?

CAT'S FUNERAL by E. V. Rieu

> Bury her deep, down deep,
> Safe in the earth's cold keep,
> Bury her deep —
>
> No more to watch bird stir;
> No more to clean dark fur;
> No more to glisten as silk;
> No more to revel in milk;
> No more to purr.
>
> Bury her deep, down deep;
> She is beyond warm sleep.
> She will not walk in the night;
> She will not wake to the light.
> Bury her deep.

By Karl Fletcher, aged 11

CAT CAT
A SMALL
THING
NICE SOFT
FLUFFY
FUR
SOME LONG
THIN WISKERS.
FROM ITS WET
SMALL NOSE, TWO
CUDDLY EYES AND
A MOUTH WITH SMALL
SHARP TEETH, FOUR
SMALL SKINNY
LEGS WITH
FOUR FL-
ABBY PAWS THE BOTTOM

STRAY KITTEN by Margaret Greaves

Witch-kitten!
Thin!
Where have you been?
Leaf-blown and light on the garden wall,
Ice-green and star-bright your flickering gaze,
Witch-kitten, can you tell nothing at all
Of the rides by night and the magical days
That you dance to remember, high up on the wall?
Mocking and thin,
Blacker than sin,
Kitten from nowhere, that won't come in—
Witch-kitten, witch-kitten,
Where have you been?

Used together with the above poems were:

CATS SLEEP ANYWHERE by Eleanor Farjeon
FIVE EYES by Walter de la Mare
THE CAT by W. H. Davies
INSIDE by Eleanor Fargeon
THE LOST CAT by E. V. Rieu
TIGER-TIGER by William Blake
TO AN OLD CAT by Jillian Perry, aged 8.

Sources for all these poems can be found in Appendix A.

Janet Ede with Joan Varley

Mixed ability class of 9-10 year-olds

When a number of project teachers invited me into their schools to take a poetry session with children I was apprehensive, to say the least, and agonized for some time about whether I could do it after an absence of twelve years from the classroom, and about which poems I would choose. The account which follows is a description of a particular session I planned with Joan Varley at Brockwell Junior School on the theme of 'Cats', which I had tried in other schools. Because of the nature of my college work it was not possible to visit the school on a regular basis, so Joan and I planned that I should introduce the theme in a morning session and she would follow up and develop the ideas.

I felt that the theme of 'Cats' offered a number of possibilities. Many children possess cats as pets and they are, therefore, familiar and loved. Many children would like to possess a kitten. It is also a theme which can lend itself to the mysterious, e.g. 'Tiger' and 'Stray Kitten', which is pictured as a witch kitten, 'light as a blown leaf'. There is something mysterious and secretive about some cats: in Comic and Curious Cats,[11] a book of paintings and poems, there is a marvellous painting of a cat called Dominic. There he sits, with his midnight-black fur frosted with silver, and his amber staring eyes. It is a wonderful tactile painting.

There is a wide range of poems available on the 'Cat' theme. Of course not all were used (or would be) on each occasion, but they are available. It is a case of picking the right ones to suit the particular occasion and the response of the pupils. The poems vary in the demands they make on the pupils — 'Tiger' is the most challenging both in language and ideas; 'Cat's Funeral' is in its own way a masterpiece and reminds me of some of Emily Bronte's poems on death. I love the sonorous monosyllables of 'Safe in the earth's cold keep . . .'. It is language which stretches use and meaning: 'keep' — safekeeping, castles, towers, dungeons, prisoners.

Other poems I chose because they were by other children. It's always as well to let a class know it isn't only the adults who can write poems! I also looked at a variety of poetic techniques — Karl's shape poem and Eleanor Farjeon's 'Cat' with its staccato tempo.

I began by asking whether the children had cats. What like? Names? Tricks? Then I moved straight into Comic and Curious Cats. I showed the group 'Dominic' who 'daringly eats dragees and lives in Diss'. We simply enjoyed the picture; the words we read but didn't tease out for meaning. Then on to kitten poems from the selection and we talked about the playfulness of cats and kittens. 'Miss Tibbles' and 'Stray Kitten' both create the movement of young cats — 'she moves in little gusts and breezes', and we talked about contrast in the way young and old cats move and the words used to describe them.

Then we went on to Karl's shape poem, 'Cats'. This is by someone their age, and the shape does offer some guide to the language to be used. It is a framework which some children need as guidance when they write. We looked at the clever way Karl had chosen words of a suitable length to fill the different parts of the body such as the ears and tail. Then we looked at the two contrasting pictures of 'The Cat' by W. H. Davies, as it appears in two different anthologies, and decided which picture best fitted the poem.

Then we moved on to poems to say together — 'Old Cat', 'Cats Sleep Anywhere' and 'Cat'. In our efforts not to embarrass children we've stopped asking them to read aloud, and choral speech is no longer fashionable. As a result we've given children no chance to try the words for themselves. We, the adults, take on the reading and the enjoyment. But, surely, one of the important ways in which we learn to appreciate language is to try it out for ourselves — not silently taking it in by sight but saying it aloud, and savouring all its power to evoke and create a mood within us. So — let's say the poems together. This way we'll support the poor reader. Poems can be split up round the class; groups of children can work as a chorus; they can even chant individual words they like. Of course, this can be worked up into choral speech and performance, but the emphasis should be on enjoyment and not on a perfect rendering.[12]

There is a value in letting children enjoy the sound. I discovered this at Eastwood when I did similar work with another class. They picked out favourite words and we said them together. It is surprising how they gain confidence very quickly and join in spontaneously. In Talking, writing and learning 8-13,[13] emphasis is laid on the ways in which we can help children 'grow' into literature so that they can take it to themselves with meaning. One suggestion is that selecting and saying the words of the text can be a step on the road to being able to discuss in detail one's responses to literature. I believe this is true also for poetry.

I saved 'The Lost Cat', 'Cat's Funeral' and 'Tiger' until last, when I had the measure of the children and knew a little more about their responses. All of these do <u>need</u> to be read by a teacher — read and then left with all the weight of their language making its own point. I did discuss them with one of my groups but felt the discussion was an anti-climax.

Joan and I considered what experiences the children might encounter in this work.

(1) *Listening* to the compressed and patterned use of language in poetry. Experiencing rhyme and rhythm. Experiencing the non-literal uses of language, e.g. the cat 'light as a blown leaf'.

(2) *Talking* — comparing their own cats, and experience of cats, with cats in the poems. Picking out words they liked. Opportunities to enjoy saying some of these words alone, and as a group. Discussing which drawing etc., is most appropriate for a particular poem. Talking about their favourite 'Cat' poem — this was done in pairs. The chance to talk and make decisions — 'How shall we say this poem?'

(3) *Writing.* Using pictures of cats in 'Comic and Curious Cats', I made templates of cats and cut these out of coloured card. Children could then write their own cat poem, copy out one they liked, or write a cat ABC choosing an initial for their cat as Martin Leman does with Dominic, for example.

(4) The extension of *Reading* by motivating the children to read beyond the poems — to experience feelings which extend the frontiers of awareness into other kinds of writing such as fiction.[14]

Joan also felt that further art work would be a good idea and as follow-up work after my visit planned to make dustbins of grey corrugated card stuck on a black background which the children could decorate with dustbin material such as fish bones and tin cans — cut out of card I should add! This could be used as the background for displaying children's writing, as also could a black silhouette of roof tops and chimneys. Drama work was also planned as a follow-up using the record of the musical 'Cats'[15] as an inspiration, and asking the children to move like the cats suggested in the music. 'Old Possum's Book of Practical Cats',[16] which forms the basis of the musical was also available for teacher and pupils to read.

We were very pleased with the initial responses of the children. We spent an hour on the work and I thought they maintained their concentration very well. I felt I must vary my presentation more next time with this age group — puppets perhaps. I should also have broken up the hour and given more opportunities for them to do things — physically as well as mentally. Drama could usefully have been inserted earlier I felt, and would have enhanced subsequent writing.

However both Joan and I were very pleased with the way they joined in the saying of the poems — even a boy who was rather slow joined in. The resulting collages of dustbins and poems were very effective. The teacher reported that the drama went well — 'girl' cats up trees, beseiged by 'boy' cats, hissing and scratching! And then the boys wanted to be the 'girl' cats!

Summing up the work as a whole, at one level there had been an obvious enjoyment for all of us in reading and saying the poems. The children showed a willingness to talk and to relate the poems to themselves and themselves to the poems. Enjoyment expressed in children's responses is always pleasing but we need to be wary of condemning the children who are silent. The quality of art work and writing often shows something of the responses of children who initially appear unmoved by the experience. We need to be wary of looking for the 'instant' response. Poems, in their power to evoke feelings, may work stealthily and secretly and manifest themselves in later life. Evidence for this is available in the responses of adults — the teacher I met who could remember only one poem from childhood, Wordsworth's 'Daffodils', but who could say the entire poem from memory with obvious pleasure.

The rapport which developed was exhilarating for me and, I feel, enjoyable for the children, although one can't always be sure. I also felt a sense of release because I had felt free in the classroom in a way in which I never had as a teacher. I realize, rather sadly now, that much of my teaching of poetry then was constrained by my concern that I should choose a 'good' poem (a result of my English literature degree) and that I must be seen to be 'teaching' something. It is as if my absence from the classroom has given me a perspective I lacked before. All the 'good' poems in the world will be useless if not enjoyed!

Poems should reverberate in the mind so that the words and lines stay in the memory and can be said and resaid, savoured at leisure, with the accruing experiences of life adding further depth and creating new understanding of the original. For me, many Derbyshire days are grey. Wilfred Owen's picture of the battlefields of Flanders enables me to respond to the grey days, to enjoy them even:

> Rain soaks, and clouds sag stormy
> Dawn massing in the east her melancholy army
> Attacks once more in ranks on shivering ranks of grey,
> But nothing happens.[17]

As I drive round the words echo and re-echo in my mind.

An Old Cat

> Lying on the dusty road,
> Basking in the sun,
> An old cat never has any fun,
> The old cat rises slowley,
> And slinks off down the road
> She stalks round the corner to number 43,
> And settles on her mat waiting for her tea.

by Tony, age 10

Points to Ponder

(1) The use of a group of poems considered together.

(2) The importance here of the original illustrations to poems.

(3) The importance of children trying language for themselves and becoming aware of the sound of poetry.

(4) The importance of 'language which stretches'.

(5) And the importance of other kinds of 'language'. i.e. Artwork to re-create the meaning of the poem in their own terms. Movement enabling a re-interpretation of the language of the poem in a different medium.

POEM by Hugh Sykes Davies

In the stump of the old tree, where the heart
has rotted out,/there is a hole the length of a
man's arm, and a dank pool at the/bottom of it
where the rain gathers, and the old leaves turn
into/lacy skeletons. But do not put your hand
down to see, because

in the stumps of old trees, where the hearts
have rotted out,/there are holes the length of a
man's arm, and dank pools at the/bottom where
the rain gathers and old leaves turn to lace, and
the/beak of a dead bird gapes like a trap. But do
not put your/hand down to see, because

in the stumps of old trees with rotten hearts
where the rain/gathers and the laced leaves and
the dead bird like a trap, there/are holes the
length of a man's arm, and in every crevice of
the/rotten wood grow weasels' eyes like
molluscs, their lids open/and shut with the tide.
But do not put your hand down to see, because

in the stumps of old trees where the rain
gathers and the/trapped leaves and the beak,
and the laced weasels' eyes, there are/holes the
length of a man's arm, and at the bottom a
sodden bible/written in the language of rooks.
But do not put your hand down/to see, because

in the stumps of old trees where the hearts
have rotted out there are holes the length of a
man's arm where the weasels are/trapped and
the letters of the rook language are laced on
the/sodden leaves, and at the bottom there is a
man's arm. But do/not put your hand down to
see, because

in the stumps of old trees where the hearts
have rotted out/there are deep holes and dank
pools where the rain gathers, and/if you ever put
your hand down to see, you can wipe it in
the/sharp grass till it bleeds, but you'll never
want to eat with/it again.

Joan Varley

Mixed ability class of 9-10 year-olds

This was a poem introduced to me by another teacher and it was a poem I did not know,
but became extremely fascinated by. I felt it would appeal to my class who are very
inventive extroverts, and who get more out of 'doing' than out of analysing poems.

When I read it I could see the possibility of using the poem in an 'I went to Paris and
bought . . . ' type of game, because of the repetitive nature and building-on qualities of
the poem. I wanted each child to think up a macabre sentence/object to find in the

stump and after repeating what had gone before to add their object, going right round the class. Then after building up, it loses a line at a time, until the original line only is left. In this way we made a chanting sort of witches' rhyme.

We went down to the river to find a tree stump which would be carried back to the classroom. (We were not very successful, but found enough rotting, mouldy wood to create a stump.) This was set up on a table with long spikes of green paper to create a grassy setting. At the back of the stump I secured a sack bag for children to reach into, as if they were going down into the stump. In the bag I put a dozen labels with macabre objects on them — this was just to set the mood and give ideas.

After some good readings through, splitting up into the repetitive 'choruses', children came forward to put their hands in, while the rest of the class chanted the first and last lines. The children then each wrote a descriptive horrific sentence on a piece of paper and secretly put it in the stump. Then we went through the whole procedure again with tremendous excitement because there were thirty two new things in the stump and thirty two 'pullings out' and much chanting.

There were some specific things which I wanted to achieve:

(1) I wanted children to get the 'building up' and choruses idea and to come forward with lots of evil and dreadful things which might be found.

(2) I wanted them to think:
Why were the particular objects there? Whether they could take each one and extend it in a story or poem.

(3) I wanted them to write their own poems using the same format and the first and last lines.

(4) Choral speaking, mime and drama were other possibilities I had in mind.

The poem immediately appealed to the children, mainly because of its horrific nature. The rotting wood added to it because they could actually poke it and leap back when 'creepy crawlies' came out. The secrecy of putting in their idea appealed, and who could think up the most frightening, and who pulled out whose idea (two children actually drew out their own slips of paper).

This response was most lively — excitement, tremendous ideas. They wanted to do it over and over to anyone who came into the room — staff, visitors. Other groups I teach (sewing, maths) were also involved until the stump disintegrated, and then we used the bark to create a collage tree stump picture. Their poetry was lively too and seemed to come easily to them, because after all the repetition they knew the format and lines off by heart.

This poem lasted all one week and into the next. We became very fond of it, referring to it many times. It created for us a lovely atmosphere of adventure. The tactile experience of using a stump was worthwhile and made all the difference; it set the scene. 'Doing' and 'contributing' got it across well to the children and it came easily to them.

The poem took over and swept us along.

In the Stump of the Old Tree

In the stump of old tree, where the heart has rotted out
There is a metal bloodstained casket with an eye in it
But do not put your hand down to see, because ----

In the stump of the old tree where the heart has rotted out
There is a metal bloodstained casket with an eye in it
There is an empty skull with a candle burning brightly
But do not put your hand down to see, because - - - -

In the stump of the old tree where the heart has rotted out
There is a metal bloodstained casket with an eye in it
There is an empty skull with a candle burning brightly
There is a bloody arrow through an eyeball
But do not put your hand down because - - - -

In the stump of an old tree, where the heart has rotted out
There is a metal bloodstained casket with an eye in it
There is an empty skull with a candle burning brightly
There is a bloody arrow through an eyeball
There is a human's head with a dagger through it
But do not put your hand down because - - - -

In the stump of the old tree where the heart has rotted out
There is a metal bloodstained casket with an eye in it
There is an empty skull with a candle burning brightly
There is a bloody arrow through an eyeball
There is a human's head with a dagger through it
There is a shreveled eye with blood pouring out
But do not put your hand down to see because - - - -

In the stump of an old tree where the heart has rotted out
There is a metal bloodstained casket with an eye in it
There is an empty skull with a candle burning brightly
There is a human's head with a dagger through it
There is shreveled eye with blood pouring out
There is a rat with its gibberlets hanging out
But do not put your hand down to see because - - - -

           YOUR
              HAND
                 WILL
                    JOIN
     Beware   THEM

by Kerry, age 10

Points to Ponder

(1) The importance of 'doing' in response to poetry.

(2) Chanting and repetition. The experience of the <u>sound</u> of poetry again.

40

Marylyn Grasar

Mixed ability class of 9-11 year-olds

I have used this poem before with this age range, with a variety of positive and negative responses. I was interested to see how a class which has expressed interest and enthusiasm for many types of poetry would respond to a poem which builds up an atmosphere, and demands concentration and thought.

We decided to go into the library, a cosy, intimate atmosphere, the place most likely to be free from interruption. I began by explaining how and why I had a copy of this poem, so before hearing it the children knew it to be one of my favourites. I then read the poem to the children. After a little discussion, they all had their own copy, and we read each verse in turn, a different reader each time, with an opportunity between each verse for anyone to say anything they wished about it, ask questions, and comment upon repetitions.

I hoped that the children would show a development of their ideas about the poem as they talked about it: that they would compare and contrast this poem with an earlier poem, 'A Case of Murder' (see page 19); that they would add something to their limited knowledge of poetic methods, (verses, repetition, rhymes, etc.); that they would relate some of their own experiences of exploring dead trees and tree-stumps; that they would produce some form of written work, not necessarily a poem, and some art work.

All the children listened well, wanted to read part of it aloud, and had plenty to comment upon. They appeared quite willing to say if there was a part they wanted to talk about, or a word they did not understand. Any questions which are asked by them are usually answered by other children, but they expect answers to be from evidence given in the poem, otherwise they will say, 'We can't be sure, he doesn't tell us, but this is the most likely answer.' Of particular interest was the poet's reason for writing: had it really happened? What gave him the idea? Was it part real; part imagination? Running through their comments was the wish that explanations should be logical; how could weasel's eyes get in a tree stump? How could the dead rook have got there? How can the grass make your hand bleed? Between them, they decided that a 'sodden Bible, written in the language of rooks' was a piece of newspaper that had blown into the stump, got wet, and been picked at by the birds.

I was most impressed by their voluntary oral responses, their willingness to ask questions, and their willingness to answer questions where reference to the poem was necessary. They were willing to comment upon their feelings, and to comment upon any similar experiences. There was mention of other poems with a similar 'spooky atmosphere' (their description). A poem they remembered from infant days, 'The Dark, Dark, Wood', was recited without any encouragement from me and led on to mentions of other similar poems. When asked whether they would like to split into groups to prepare for a class reading, or write their own poems, they all decided they wanted to write first. Although keen, they were not able to produce writing which satisfied them as much as on previous occasions. About half asked if they could do more work at home, and the extra time and thought has helped them in revising and altering their original poems.

The children present were able to read the poem for themselves, join in discussion, and contribute some ideas of their own. With hindsight, I would not present this poem in the same way again. I would search for easier ways into the writing: writing in pairs; composing a class poem; choosing a verse each and changing six words; sequencing — putting words in one line in the best possible order, or re-arranging certain words, lines, or verses; cloze procedure (presenting a line or verse with some words deleted). Activities which would encourage the children to look at the structure of the poem, the word order and choice of words would help to promote confidence in their own ability to write poetry. A tape-recording would be useful, both for listening to the poem, and for children reading the poem.

I feel that the poetry reading and discussion were successful, but the written work not up to the children's usual standard. I think I expected too much of some of them, but it has given the more able children an opportunity to work at a difficult poem.

I have noticed a general increase in the sales of poetry books in the school bookshop, and an increasing awareness of which poems can be found where. My own interest in poetry seems to have influenced a favourable attitude in most children. The less able children have shown just as much enthusiasm as the others, and show an equal interest in reading poetry.

Do Not Follow That Path Because . . .

In a very thick dense wood
Where it's very dark and creepy
There's a solitary path running
Towards the dark tangled centre
Do not follow that path because

Inside the very thick dense wood
Where it's even darker and creepy
A solitary path leads on
Nearer to the dark tangled centre
Do not follow that path because

Near the centre of a thick dense wood
Where its black and creepy crawlies
                daren't go
The solitary path gets narrower
And overgrown with brambled-tangles
Do not follow that path because

In the dense black centre of a wood
There's a hole that's a bottomless pit
Its entrance is hidden with brambles
A narrow path leads to the edge
        and . . . .

by Samantha, age 11

Points to Ponder

(1) A concern with poetic techniques, structures.

(2) The planning of activities to focus upon this.

David Bennett

Middle band ability class of 11-12 year-olds

We had previously done some work on 'Jabberwocky' (see page 22) and thought about the danger and mystery in it; the warnings inherent in 'Poem' seemed like a good development from that.

I asked the children to close their eyes and imagine an old hollow tree stump before them. Then what might be in the hollow? Next, they put their hands in and drew it out. A few pupils explained to the others what they had found, carefully choosing suitable descriptive words. On slips of paper each child secretly wrote what was in the tree stump and these were put into a box. I began a chant based on the poem, and when I stopped, a child picked out a slip and continued the chant. We then read the original duplicated poem twice, with the children automatically joining in and involving themselves, after which there followed a brief discussion on the poem's structure. In groups of four the pupils took four slips at random from the box and went away to compose and record their own chants for the rest of the class. Sound effects were encouraged. These were played back later.

As a homework pupils composed their own chants based upon a Warning such as:

(i)   Do not enter that darkened room because . . .
(ii) Do not follow that winding path because . . .
(iii) Never open that oaken door because . . .

These were displayed on a kind of large postcard with the warning emblazoned on the front and a relevant door, tree, bottle, chest or whatever which could be opened to reveal the poem behind. As an offshoot of this I persuaded the music department to help the children to put some of their chants to music in their music lessons, which were used in a school concert.

The children revelled in the mystery and intrigue in the poem. They learnt, I am sure, from the controlled repetition and manipulation of language, which most managed to reproduce in their own work. I saw one girl in the school bookshop busily reading her poem to a friend from another class, both joining in the repetitive chant.

The various possibilities and modes of work that emerged from the poem proved a surprise and delight to us all, especially the opening doors, which prompted considerable creative excitement and involvement for both writer and reader. Similarly the drama; and the co-operation with another subject area (music) was a less usual and therefore particularly challenging departure.

Undoubtedly the poem holds an excitement and interest for children which can be extended into many areas of activity. Further drama or story work that I might have done was curtailed by the arrival of the end of term. Weaving these chants into a long adventure story or play would seem like a useful line to follow in the future, since children occasionally need the experience of sustaining thoughts and ideas over a longer period; this piece could be a useful springboard.

I also employed this poem with a fourth year O-level group. They were visibly overcome by its impact, appreciating immediately its complexity and form. Their reaction was so positive that they were itching to try writing their own warnings. I allowed them only thirty minutes to do so and the results were, in the main, stunning. These were then presented for display in any way that the pupils chose — as a result of which I had coffins which opened, pop-up magic gardens and exploding parcels with dire messages attached!

Do Not Open This Door Because

At the bottom of these steps
sits an old woman,
with thoughts of an older world,
and she wishes not to be disturbed, so . . .

Do not open this door,
for there sits a woman of an older world,
surrounded by dust and darkness,
and the remnants of a past age,
unchanged by the new, so . . .

Do not open this door,
for there in the dark room at the bottom
                              of the stairs,
is a frail old woman, but
do not disturb her for she will not
                              answer you,
She has returned to her age gone by.

by Martin, age 14

Points to Ponder

(1) The controlled repetition and manipulation of language.

(2) The use of chanting and chants (the sound of poetry again).

(3) The setting of the chants to music.

(4) Three very different and individual accounts of the teaching of the same poem.

FOLLOWER by Seamus Heaney

My father worked with a horse-plough,
His shoulders globed like a full sail strung
Between the shafts and the furrow.
The horses strained at his clicking tongue.

An expert. He would set the wing
And fit the bright steel-pointed sock.
The sod rolled without breaking.
At the headrig, with a single pluck

Of reins, the sweating team turned round
And back into the land. His eye
Narrowed and angled at the ground,
Mapping the furrow exactly.

I stumbled in his hob-nailed wake,
Fell sometimes on the polished sod;
Sometimes he rode me on his back
Dipping and rising to his plod.

I wanted to grow up and plough,
To close one eye, stiffen my arm.
All I ever did was follow
In his broad shadow round the farm.

I was a nuisance, tripping, falling,
Yapping always. But today
It is my father who keeps stumbling
Behind me, and will not go away.

Joan Varley

Mixed ability class of 9-10 year-olds

This seemed a hard poem for my children, I thought, as I read it to myself, because my class seem better at 'doing' than analysing. I felt that a picture was needed and I came across a sheet of wrapping paper with lots of exactly the pictures the poem was describing. Thus I was able to make up an attractive card with the picture and the poem side by side, for every child in the class. Because of the 'difficulty' of the poem I led into it very gradually and gently. We read it in parts, to ourselves, out loud, silently and discussed it in general terms, then left it for a day or two.

To fill in some social background I dipped into Lark Rise to Candleford[18] by Flora Thompson, which has excellent passages about life in the fields, food, clothing, conversations, wives, housing conditions. The children really enjoyed this and when we returned to the poem on another day they felt more familiar with it and seemed to enjoy the atmosphere, recognising the country scenes. And I used The Country Diary of an Edwardian Lady.[19]

I was very lucky to get a lot of ploughing equipment, blades, plough harrows, coulters, mouldboards, and some first-hand information from an expert. My class loved this and we lugged the heavy farming equipment all over and had it on display in the classroom. Without labouring it too much I made up a booklet of questions asking what they liked, understood, didn't understand, phrases to discuss, landscape, the farmer, the boy, the mother watching. There was a lot of work in the booklet and some got bogged down.

I had the following activities in mind:
1. Some descriptive writing:
   (a) as the boy, or
   (b) as the father, or
   (c) as a mother taking food out to them, or
   (d) as a scarecrow.
2. To find out about other rural crafts.
3. To discuss on tape.
4. To write a poem called: 'A day's work', or 'Ploughing', or 'The Team'.
5. Art work: clay modelling of a horse and plough; collage landscape work, horse brasses; rubbings; sketching ploughing equipment.

The children responded with a quiet enthusiasm, but it was heavy going until we actually got something tangible, e.g. agricultural equipment. Then horse-brasses came from home. They said they enjoyed it because it was in the country, and they said the poem was good at making them picture the scene exactly. When the ploughing equipment was in the classroom it seemed to mean more to them just from the shapes of the blades that turn the earth over. And they talked about it a lot. But I was conscious of always having to remind them to think about the poem and its meaning and they found the language strange in parts. Rural children would have been more at one with the language, the technical terms. I would have liked to have gone to a ploughed field, but the field and time were not available. Perhaps it was because the poem was 'quiet' that the response was quiet; there was not a lot of scope for lively mime or drama.

They all enjoyed all the activities involved with it, the craft, the rubbings, horse-brasses, social life, history, background, but I think they found the 'analysing' of it difficult. They wrote some good descriptive poetry, really re-creating the mood and atmosphere. They discussed it on tape extremely well, having organized themselves without my presence (see page 71).

There was a point when I felt I was overdoing it and had to leave it and come back to it after a while, otherwise they might have finished up hating poetry for ever more! The break was refreshing for me too and then further good work was produced.

I felt that once started we had to see it through, but more so because it was for a special reason. Normally if something does not go well I would abandon it, after rounding it off prematurely, and try something else. Not everything one does is a roaring success, one just learns to recognize this and accept it for what it is, and try another tack.

A Day's Work

A day's work is done
I've done some sowing the seeds
Now it's time to have something to eat
a drink of wine and some bread and lard
But First I must wash, am black on
My Face am black on my arms and hands
its a really hot day for working

by David, age 9

Points to Ponder

(1) 'Doing' rather than analysing. (Is there a feeling somewhere that one ought to 'analyse' the poem, but that children find this difficult? Or perhaps they simply see it as irrelevant?)

(2) Again the need for the teacher to be widely read so that she can draw on appropriate material.

(3) With a 'difficult' poem, the need for some concrete focal points. i.e. the pictures and later the ploughing equipment.

Eveline Fullwood

Mixed ability class of 9-11 year-olds

I kept putting off the presentation of this poem because it seemed to fit into nothing else I was doing, and I like to slot my poetry into other work if at all possible. Then, a fortnight ago, we had an exchange of library books and one of the children chose a book with a beautiful picture of a farmer working with a horse plough. This gave me the opportunity I had been waiting for. We discussed the picture and the old way of ploughing; the skill of the farmer; and this led on to talk about other country crafts:
  (a)   Thatching — we have a thatcher in the village, but no thatched roofs!
  (b)   Dry stone-walling — a feature of our part of the country and a sight with which the children are familiar.
  (c)   Hedging — also a familiar sight to the children.
I then gave the children copies of the poem which I read to them. They found it difficult to understand, but after a second reading, and reading it by themselves, it became easier. The children enjoyed the poem even though 'it doesn't rhyme', 'one verse joins on to another one'. I felt that the poem had been successful, even though I thought it was difficult for my children, especially the less able.

The children were immediately interested in ploughing and found reference books from the library, and from home; group discussions were held about old and modern methods of ploughing and the advantages and disadvantages of one over the other. We used the reference library and found an illustration of a plough and a ploughed field, and from this we found the meaning of the 'heading', the 'wing' and the 'sock'. As we discovered the meanings of these 'new' words the children's understanding of the poem became much clearer and their interest increased. They thought the description of the farmer following the plough — 'His shoulders globed like a full sail strung Between the shafts and the furrow' — was very good: 'He would look like a ship's sail,' they said, 'especially if there was a bit of wind, and it was blowing his coat out a bit as well.'

They talked about their parents' work and whether they would like to follow them. We discussed other kinds of following: pop stars, football teams, the disciples following Jesus — these were all the children's own ideas. Some of the children, interested in the stars, related the poem to the constellation, The Plough, and found and read a story about The Great Bear.

I was open to any suggestions for work the children might make but I also wanted poems from the children themselves. We followed all these varied and interesting discussions with art work and the writing of their own poems. Some of the children found this rather difficult, but they succeeded in interpreting the poem in terms of their own lives, their hopes and aspirations.

I found, on reflection, that both the children and I had derived great benefit from this shared experience — the poem was new to me, as well as to them — and what I had at first thought to be an almost impossible poem to do with them, turned out to be a very pleasurable and interesting exercise. The moral here is surely 'have a go'; because had it not been for the poetry project I would never have attempted this poem with my class, considering it far too difficult for them to understand. Perhaps we often underestimate our children's ability. The discussions and the poems they produced showed their understanding, and gave them a sense of achievement — having tackled successfully something which at the beginning they had found difficult.

Following

Many people follow
Different sorts of creed,
Many thousands follow
But only a few can lead

Some follow "United"
Some follow "The Blues"
They'll keep on following
Win or Lose

Many will follow England
On the road to Spain
Hoping when they get there
They'll win all their games

It's easy to follow somebody
Who's going along the wrong way
But it's harder to do the right thing
Day after day after day

by Mark, age 10

Points to Ponder

(1) The pleasure of the shared experience of the teacher and the children.

David Bennett

Upper band ability class of 13-14 year-olds

This is not a poem which I personally would have chosen. The work which emerged was a very pleasant surprise.

I had been asked to use this poem with a class. I presented duplicated copies to the group and asked them to discuss it in pairs for ten minutes, after which I would answer questions. As usual I managed to re-route the pupils' questions to me so that another pupil answered and that way the poem was more satisfactorily examined and explained, largely on the pupils' own terms, not by a formula for discussion pre-set by the teacher.

A homework was set — write a ten-fifteen line appreciation of the poem thinking about (a) its theme, (b) the way in which the poet wrote it and (c) your feelings about the poem (see page 86). A selection of photocopies of the pupils' work was collected into a booklet called 'Responses to a Poem' and displayed, along with the original, in the library.

The day after this I was in discussion with other members of the project and an idea for using this poem with one of my first year classes was formulated in my mind.

I wrote the two words 'The Follower', on a clean blackboard and asked the pupils to think in silence for two minutes and decide what those words meant to them personally. There followed ideas like ghosts, Christ and his disciples, following a team or pop group, spies and criminals, special investigators, tracking, etc., etc. The last offering was 'following parents' which led us neatly into the poem. I read it once and then invited offers from the class to read it, which was done. Then I told the class that I wanted them to decide in pairs what they wanted to ask me. I gave them ten minutes.

The questions that followed were taken in two sections: firstly, which individual words were causing problems, and then ideas that were difficult. A very thorough investigation ensued whereby I merely channelled questions through the chair. When asked whether they liked working this way, most concurred that they did. A few, however, decided that understanding and talking about a poem took the mystery out of it!

The activity which followed was to use one of their ideas for the follower in a piece of writing. The class decided that they would write acrostics, diaries, stories, descriptions and plays. Then came the news that they were to take their shoes and socks off and draw around their two feet in their English books. The area covered by their feet was all the space that they had for their piece of writing — (eccentric precis?!). The finished and marked pieces were copied onto bright foot-shaped pieces of card which then trailed all across a wall and up and over a ceiling in a corridor, which delighted the children hugely — Sir has really flipped his lid this time!

However, it is cranky display which arrests attention and gets noticed, not just by the perpetrators but by everyone. English used in this way, lifted out of the exercise book into the environment, is English that is concerned with involvement and excitement. This is what we ought to be doing if we are to make our subject alive and vital to our pupils. Our best friends should be the art and music departments, not just when we want to put on a play, but all the year through. An intelligently displayed piece of work reaches an audience far wider, and in many senses far more important to the writer and his progress in the subject, than the teacher.

The Follower

She follows me everyday
And drags along on my arm
all day
She's a real pain in the
neck
But I don't tell her
She'll cause an earth
quake
Well not quite
As I walk down
the street
She's there I hear
her calling
Before I answer
She's shouting
Wait for me I
want to
Come

I can't go anywhere
without her
I give hints that I don't
like her
But she doesn't seem
to realize
I just wish I could
get away
Even just for a day
It would make a
great deal of a
change
I wish I had
courage
To turn round and
tell her to go
But all I would
hear is
What's the matter
with you
Over again

by Maria, age 11

Points to Ponder

(1) 'English . . . is concerned with involvement and excitement.'

(2) Links with art and music again!

Marylyn Grasar

Mixed ability class of 9-11 year-olds

I teach in the infant department of a small primary school. Twice a week the teacher of the older juniors and I change classes. When I was asked to join the poetry network project it seemed a good opportunity to use my time with the juniors to seek to promote their interest in poetry. The Poetry Group decided to use the same poem in a variety of schools. Thus the poem was chosen for me, but how to use it was entirely my own choice. Many of my decisions were greatly influenced by timetable requirements. I had the class for half an hour on Tuesday mornings and one hour on Thursday afternoons. Anticipating that most of the class would find the poem difficult, because of its unfamiliar content and vocabulary, I hoped to promote their understanding and enjoyment by first considering relationships between parents and children, and the life of a working horse.

Tuesday 4th May
We began by discussing why it is sometimes helpful to prepare for a poem before reading it. We talked about parents who work at home, and common experiences soon became

apparent. Most children wanted to help, but ended up hindering. Every child had some incident to relate. When a group of girls asked if they could write a poem, I suggested a story for those who would prefer this, as previous experience had indicated that many of the children who show enthusiasm verbally cannot sustain this interest when faced with writing their own poem. A couple of children regarded the writing as a chore, but most wrote with speed and competence.

Thursday 6th May

Those who finished the previous day's work quickly then wrote about helping mum at home; most chose a poem rather than a story. These first two pieces of written work were, for most children, the ones in which they displayed most talent, had the least difficulty, and indicated the most enjoyment. They could write from their own experience, they did not have to imagine themselves in an unfamiliar situation, the vocabulary they needed was at their fingertips, the content of their written work was easily within their grasp, so they could concentrate on language and presentation. Similar attitudes towards parents were evident: the children's realization that they do get in the way, pester parents, and so provoke anger; amusement at the various ways lots of dads seek to avoid housework — 'My dad has an excuse that all the family knows about, he says he's taking the dog for a walk then he pops into the pub for a quick pint of beer;' and an appreciation of the way in which parents teach them by letting them help.

Catherine wrote her poem with the intention of amusing the reader, but what appeals to me is the feeling of deep appreciation for mum and all she does for her family.

Mum's Work

Zoom goes the sewing machine,
Click click goes the handle round and round.
Millions of kuts are made in one night,
Still she gets in two cups of coffee,
A sweater for dad finished in a week.
    How does she get it done?
But still she finds time to jabber away
With my auntie or a friend.
Every morning she's up at the crack of dawn,
Makes the breakfast and has a wash,
Hoovering in the morning, polishing later on,
    Dinner, then gardening,
Still the dinner is ready when I get home.

Sally attempted a rhyming poem.

Dad's Work

My dad and his mate are in the building trade.
When bricks are laid and wages are paid
He comes home and has his dinner,
Keeps on saying he's getting thinner.
At home he does odd jobs in the house,
But when there's pots to be washed
He's quiet as a mouse.

Andrew chose a prose response. He watches mum at home.

> 'She's taught me a lot but sometimes I learn just by watching my mum.
> Like a few years back I watched my mum make a cup of tea and now I
> can do it all perfectly by myself.'

Tuesday 11th May

One horse-owning girl had previously displayed horse equipment and explained its use at an assembly. The class had also written 'horse poems' and read 'horse stories' with their own teacher. This knowledge was helpful when we began to discuss the life of a working horse. Everyone had something to contribute, and most had seen a working horse: police horses, the local rag and bone man's horse-pulled cart, Chatsworth farm, agricultural shows, tourist centres, and on farms in Ireland where some children had been for holidays with relations. One question which came up this lesson was — would a farmer with a horse-drawn plough have worn boots or wellingtons?

Thursday 13th May

We looked at three duplicated extracts from books of an autobiographical type. Poor readers had difficulty with these. The first extract, from Cider With Rosie,[20] emphasizes the importance of the working horse. The other two extracts were from The Country Child.[21] The first highlights the rhythm of the seasons, and the second describes a ploughing scene.

    Most children demonstrated their interest by looking closely for clues to help with meaning, and answering one another's questions by referring to the text. (Longer episodes from these books would be suitable as class stories.) I had prepared a questionnaire about horses, to give children an opportunity of recording their ideas from the previous lesson, e.g. jobs working horses used to do, where you might see a working horse now, words to describe a working horse. They used this questionnaire as a time-filler if they had a few minutes to spare at the end of a lesson.

Tuesday 18th May

At last! The poem itself. Each child had a copy, I read it to them once. The response was enthusiastic, so many children wanted to say something. Charlotte asked how a ploughman's lunch got its name, Jason remarked upon a picture of a horse and plough on a pickle jar, several mentioned working horses on TV adverts. Most pleasing of all was Patrick's response — 'It's all about growing up and how things change.' Patrick's written work has been almost non-existent, although he has displayed so much effort and creativity that I have great hopes of him becoming a poetry reading adult. Most children asked sensible, intelligent questions about how a plough works and what a farmer does.

Thursday 20th May

Since four children had been missing for the previous lesson, we began by reading the poem again. They made discoveries about the structure of the poem when they tried to read it aloud, verse by verse. Then each child chose a favourite word, phrase, and verse. Previous experience had shown that some children will select the parts of the poem they find most difficult, thus providing a suitable opportunity for further discovery. Invariably, some children have several favourites, and others spontaneously offer reasons for their choice. This game-like activity seems to help the children to look closely at the words, and with this poem, the reading posed very few difficulties for less able readers. I then asked for some written response, either story or poem. About half needed no help, deciding quickly to be father, or son, or horse, etc. The other half needed help in getting started, content, layout, and spelling, and a few needed so much support that it was probably too difficult a task for them.

Thursday 27th May

Most finished off written work, and a front cover for their booklet on 'Follower'. I had previously seen all children in turn at lunch hours to look at their work with them, discuss how they wanted to set out their poem or story, and where to do illustrations. This would have been disastrous in class-time with these particular children.

We had time towards the end of the lesson to hear poems and stories read aloud. Children who used rhyme did so effectively; they did not use made-up or inappropriate words. Mandy wrote:

> I used to be the expert and plough my fields all day,
> but now I'm in the armchair and that's where I'll stay.

Andrew was one of only a few who used the poetic convention of inverting a phrase:

> he mumbles and groans,
> and groans and mumbles.

Lee's prose response typified their appreciation of the patience shown by a child to a parent, ' "You just go indoors and have a cup of tea," I said positively.'

Clare is a child who writes poetry with ease, yet on this occasion she preferred a story. I include this as I consider it one of the most competent and creative responses.

Our Country Farm

Our family had always been proud, proud of our farm and its country setting; the crows flew and nested in the chimney-pots and jackdaws called over the valley. My father worked with a team of horses ploughing the endless acres of fields, sowing and reaping; he was a hard-working man. My brother and I loved to run down the cowslip field and paddle in the shallow brook. Our strong heavy horses were friendly animals. They worked their long hours without a nasty look all day. My father was a perfect example of craftsmanship. He could plough a field like I could draw a straight line. The horses came in sweating every day, those hard-working steeds deserved their rest and food. When it was a fine day my favourite fancy was to follow him and ask questions all day long. Sometimes, only sometimes though, he'd let me ride on a horse's back as they plodded on their unending track. When I grew up I would sometimes boast and say, 'I'm going to plough.' But my dad said, 'No! girls don't plough.' But one day I'll plough, I'll make sure of that.

Had time and school organization permitted, there are a few ideas I would have used to extend our work on 'Follower':

(1) <u>Places to visit</u> — a country pub for a ploughman's lunch; a country park for a ride on a horse; a brewery which still uses horses and dray to deliver beer; the local blacksmith; the area where Alison Uttley lived; an agricultural show; a local farm; a ploughed field.

(2) <u>Displays</u> — horse equipment, Dinky toy models of farm equipment, books, pictures, etc.

(3) <u>Things to do</u> — children reading their poems and stories on to tape for other classes to hear; having a poetry reading for another class, the whole school, parents.
Collect poems about horses, craftsmen, experts, parents and children.
Use other Heaney poems from <u>Death of a Naturalist</u>, e.g. 'Black-berry Picking', 'Mid-term Break', 'Trout', and extracts from 'At a Potato Digging'.

Throughout the project I have tried not to treat any of the work as a 'grand spectacular', and have not spent much more time in preparation than would the ordinary class teacher doing poetry with her own class. Extracts from children's work have not been chosen because I considered them to be the best, but because they were good for that particular child.

I feel one or two children gained very little from our time together. My main difficulty lay with the more able but disruptive child. Those remedial children who were with me for every lesson managed very well and joined the discussions. I was very careful not to press them for written work, in case they should come to regard poetry as a chore. Most children came to me with a pro-poetry attitude, and have demonstrated their continuing interest by buying poetry books from the bookshop, choosing them from the library, and selecting endless 'favourite poems' to read aloud to the rest of the class.

The children's responses to 'Follower' will have some influences on my own approaches to teaching poetry, particularly with older less-able juniors. I will be more satisfied with, more enthusiastic about, and place more emphasis on verbal, dramatic and artistic responses. Such responses can be as valid and important as written responses, and just as likely to lead to a greater awareness and enjoyment of poetry. Children who are keen to write poetry can and should be given appropriate help, but those for whom poetry writing is a chore will not become poetry lovers by being compelled to write poetry. They can be led gently!

This requires a long-term strategy, with all staff involved, to promote actively the attitude that reading, listening to, and even writing, poetry is an enjoyable experience, and can be so for everyone. I wonder how many teachers would be satisfied with their own contribution to the build-up of a 'pro-poetry' attitude within their school?

When asked, 'What would you consider is a suitable poem for your class?', I think the the simplest answer is: one that I like myself and can therefore demonstrate some personal involvement with.

This poetry project has communicated one clear message to me — if children can and are willing, to write poetry, great; if they can't, or won't, don't give up, don't despair, and above all, don't panic.

My Dad the Expert

> My father was an expert
> A ploughman on the farm.
> He worked all day with horses
> And never let me have a try.
>
> He said I was a nuisance
> Tripping, falling, yapping all the time
> And never stopping, so that
> My father could not get a word in
> To talk about the plough.
> He groomed the horses

and worked the plough
And never let me have a try.

He fed them when they needed food,
But why oh why wouldn't he let me try
To feed the shires day or night
But now it's me and I
Won't let him try.

by Charlotte, age 11

3   POETRY PLATFORMS

The contributions of project members in this chapter take us beyond the detailed consideration of the teaching of individual poems into broader aspects of poetry work which are an inevitable outcome of a concern for poetry and its place in the life of a school:

(1)   They describe the various ways in which project members were able to draw in other staff in their schools through concerts, dramatic presentations, readings in assembly, and the sharing of a loan collection of poetry books, so that the work became active, on-going, in-service work;

(2)   They consider the role of agencies such as the school bookshop and the school library service in creating an interest in poetry and promoting a receptive atmosphere in which poetry work of all kinds can flourish;

(3)   They indicate the relationship of poetry to other aspects of the curriculum such as art and project work;

(4)   They acknowledge the importance of poetry in developing other language skills such as talk;

(5)   They consider poetry in the specific context of the secondary school, where the appreciation of poetry, which has been one of the joys of the primary age range, has to be developed and made more critically reflective as pupils move towards examination work.

Some of the items are of general interest, such as 'Compiling a Magazine of Children's Poetry.' Others, like 'Building a Poetry Pyramid,' are concerned with work for a specific age range; this piece discusses the important and neglected issue of planning a developmental scheme for teaching poetry to pupils from the first to the fifth years in the secondary school.

It would be a loss to any reader who chose to read only those articles dealing with his/her own teaching age range, because a great deal of what has been written is of valuable general interest. In some instances the more flexible organization of the primary school, its size and the relative ease with which a smaller number of staff can share ideas, undoubtedly makes it easier to create an atmosphere conducive to poetry work of all kinds. The size of many secondary schools, the difficulty of knowing about the work of colleagues, busy behind closed classroom doors, the increasing anxiety expressed by staff, pupils and parents about examination success, make the creation of a favourable environment for poetry work and an enjoyment of poetry for its own sake more difficult to achieve.

It is, however, easy to be trapped into a negative attitude, to feel that because schools have been organized in a certain way, with certain ends in mind, they must always be organized in that way. The experience of project members has, with few exceptions, shown that in many instances the goodwill of colleagues in attempting something new is there. In fact, very often they are delighted with a move to inject fresh ideas into what can be stultifying routine.

We hope that a 'spirit of adventure' will be the attitude in which much of this chapter is explored, with a will to see what can be done and to reflect on how poetry work may be developed and extended in one's own school.

Poetry for Pleasure

A presentation of poems through choral speech and drama, by junior pupils

Eveline Fullwood

Inspired by the work another member of the project had done to involve all the staff in her school in poetry, I thought I would try to devise something that would involve both staff and children in the junior department of my school.

After much thought I came up with the idea of a 'Poetry for Pleasure' afternoon, at which each class in the junior school would present a poem to the rest of the school. As the idea took shape I decided to extend the audience and the invitation to include the infants, the kitchen staff, the ancillary helpers, the school secretary and several people who come into the school to help in various ways, thus making the venture a little bit more of an occasion.

As nothing like this had ever been done in the school previously, I was a little apprehensive as to how the idea would be received by the rest of the staff, and was prepared with poems and ideas if these were necessary. The staff, who knew that I was working on the poetry project, gave me their wholehearted support, and so the planning went ahead.

The final selection of poems was made by staff and pupils − the latter showing an awareness of the need to present a varied programme with both humorous and serious poems. The first year juniors chose 'Engineers',[22] an appropriately short poem for this age group with plenty of opportunity for movement and noises to convey the working of the machinery. In this, as in all the poems, there was no attempt at scenery, only token costumes and some props. Too great an emphasis on an over-elaborate production can inhibit pupils.

'The Marrog'[23] was presented through choral speech, the group of children dominated by a huge Marrog made in craft from card and glittering paper and supported on a frame of sticks, showing 'the body of brass and twenty-four fingers and toes'.

Upper juniors performed two poems. 'My Mother saw a Dancing Bear'[24] was chosen by pupils who were fully aware of the sadness of the bear's plight as it was made to 'caper in the summer heat'. Upper juniors also sustained a fuller dramatization of 'Mrs Malone'.[25] This is a long poem and was presented mainly by individual speakers accompanied by mime.

It was decided to keep the whole performance to a twenty-thirty minute period, as I felt this was quite long enough for the other children, especially the infants, to sit and watch. There was also the question of how much time we were to devote to the preparation, because there is always the danger of something like this 'taking over' too much of class time. We therefore decided to keep time spent on preparation to a minimum; similarly for the rehearsals in the hall, which is also a classroom and dinner room. The first year juniors did not use the hall at all until the actual performance.

The third and fourth years made and decorated individual invitation cards so that there was one for each child in the infant department and also one for all the other people we invited. The teacher of the reception class used these invitations as the basis for a lesson, and the children made a large and colourful acceptance card which they all signed.

The afternoon was an unparalleled success giving great pleasure to both watchers and performers. The whole school was involved in one way or another and the amount of writing, art and craft which came out of the venture was amazing in variety, content and quantity. The whole undertaking was a very worthwhile experience, and for many children it aroused a greater interest in poetry — this being shown by the number of poetry books which were borrowed from the library and my own class poetry corner, as well as my own personal collection being used and books brought from home.

Subsequently we were able to visit the TV unit at Matlock College (an experience in itself) and video the production. This has been shown to parents and used as the basis of a parents' evening.

The afternoon was such a success that we decided that we would repeat a similar experience perhaps once a term. Any effort we can make which will arouse in children an interest in the often forgotten pleasure of poetry is surely well worthwhile.

Poetry Week at George Spencer

A variety of activities in a comprehensive school focused on poetry
and drawing together pupils and staff from many departments.

David Bennett

The English department has fallen into the pattern of organizing at least one event per term. Productions so far had included book fairs, school plays, handwriting competitions and some participation in school musical concerts. Now the idea of a poetry week in the spring term was suggested. As usual the original concept of a simple affair mushroomed into a production of epic proportions!

The two main priorities were to involve the rest of the staff and the children. Then came the participation of parents. Flattery and downright bullying helped us in the first instance. The headmaster, two deputies, the director of a curriculum development unit on our site, the head of science and the librarian were all coerced into talking about and reading their 'Desert Island Poems'. Then the heads of art and music were told that they ought to assist on a point of reciprocal honour, so an illustrated competition was arranged and poems were set to music by first and second years. Finally, the modern languages department agreed to 'do something' on French and German poems; and the home economics staff undertook to arrange refreshments.

Obviously all of this material would form a programme for a 'Poetry Concert', but some build-up was necessary to involve as many pupils as possible in the initial stages. Here the English department sprang into action. We are an 11-16 comprehensive with approximately 850 pupils, and it was decided to aim poetry week at first-third years, who represented the comprehensive intake to date. Every pupil entered the verse speaking and the handwriting competition and the staff persuaded more or less everyone to enter the verse writing competition. In all cases separate poems or topics were chosen for each year and first, second and third prizes were donated by the headmaster. After the English staff's initial selection the final adjudication was by a local poet. She agreed to come to the concert, not only to read her own work, but to judge the finals of the verse speaking.

The final strands came together with the drama club's dramatization of 'The Pied Piper', some pupils' success in local and national poetry competitions (the authors of which read their poems) and several weeks of concentrated poetry work in English, which generated exemplary interest amongst staff and pupils, besides volumes of display material.

The evening was as well attended as any of the Musical Soirées for which the school is renowned. Invitations had gone to all parents. We told them that there was to be a 7.15 p.m. start, a quarter of an hour before our intended beginning, which gave time for browsing around the displays and the Poetry Bookshop, for refreshments and for putting paid to latecomers. In a continued informal atmosphere the programme ran for an hour and a half. Proceeds from a collection at the door and from the sale of a small school poetry anthology went towards a Poetry Collection for the library.

Was 'Poetry Week' like 'The Week of the Blind' — salving our consciences that that's our bit done for a while? For the hundred or so children directly involved I think not; for the confidence in poetry that it gave staff, I think not; and finally, from the references to the week that I still hear and the pupils' openness to poetry, I think not. Such results are unmeasurable, like all things that are to do with attitudes and responses to learning, but that does not prevent us from feeling that they are results worthy of the original undertaking. Our problem is how to follow that!

Spreading the Poetic Message

Poems presented in a fortnight's assemblies by staff and pupils

Joan Varley

Brockwell Junior School, where I teach, is a very open, friendly place, and when I embarked upon the Schools' Council poetry project most of my colleagues were interested in what I was doing, so in many ways it was easy for me to involve them: not because they are particularly interested in poetry, but because they like something new, a challenge, and will 'have a go' at anything.

It started as a poetry week, but continued for a fortnight and took the form of morning assemblies when themes for each day were followed. All the staff sat at the front in a semi-circle in the easy chairs from the staff room. Some days staff read their favourite poems, like a 'Desert Island Discs' idea, saying why they had chosen particular poems.

To begin with, not all the staff wanted to partake, leaving it to the extroverts, but as the days went on and enthusiasm mounted, each member of staff came to me asking to be included in the next day's programme, either because they had remembered and found an old favourite, or because their class had 'forced' them into it by their constant 'When is it your turn?', or simply because they had been caught up in the enthusiasm.

We used music such as 'Sailing', 'Knights in White Satin', 'A Whiter Shade of Pale' (from 'Classic Rock') to link themes. 'Cats' by Andrew Lloyd Webber was of course used to introduce 'Old Possum's Practical Cats'[26] while sound effects lead us into the poems 'From a Railway Carriage'[27] and 'Cargoes'.[28] (A full list of record numbers appears in Appendix F.)

Children were asked to come forward with their favourite poems and one morning was devoted to their readings. The head, too, joined in and took one assembly, using poems from his earliest memories, through childhood to later favourites. A third year class also took one morning assembly and had as its theme 'The Circling Year', taking us through a year in poetry and music. 'The Seasons' by Vivaldi was the record chosen for this theme.

We had humorous poems, cautionary tales, and ballads; in all, a great variety. We finished the fortnight in a hilarious fashion with one member of staff who is good at dialects, reciting by heart 'Albert and the Lion' and another, also from memory, 'The Battle of Hastings'.[29]

Work on poetry was done in classrooms. All the poetry books in the school and from staff's private collections were put on display; in fact when staff had read their poems in the assemblies many had shown their favourite poetry books and talked to the children about other poems in the book, particularly stressing the qualities of the reasonably priced anthologies like Salt Sea Verse[30] and I Like This Poem[31] which are often on the school's Book Club List. A school anthology was produced as a follow-up to this week. It consisted of children's own poems under the title 'A Voyage of Discovery'.

Art work in connection with poetry was done by every class — each class depicting in some way the poems their teachers had read. So we decorated the entrance hall, corridors and the hall with Marrog masks, Trains, Cats and Snitterjipes. We called the display 'These We Have Loved'. Popularity charts and graphs showing the children's favourite poems were displayed.

A good fortnight had been had by all. 'What poems are you reading tomorrow?' asked the children; and 'It's been like a breath of fresh air' said the staff. 'We must do poetry more often'.

The Role of the School Paperback Bookshop in the Poetry Dissemination Process

David Bennett

The increased enthusiasm for the sale of books in schools has been amongst the more significant advances in English teaching in recent years. The ownership of books is now emphasized as an important incentive to reading, and this can equally as well apply to poetry as to fiction or non-fiction. Sadly, the various postal book clubs that proliferate seldom offer poetry, so we are concerned here mainly with the bookshop within the school.

It is perhaps more than coincidental that several of the most popular and imaginative paperback publishers are beginning to introduce more and more collections of verse for children into their lists, and school bookshop organizers would be failing in their duty and missing valuable opportunities if they were not to include as least a selection of these books. Poetry seen alongside everything else on offer is poetry seen as thoroughly acceptable and worthwhile reading material for all members of the school community. Even if it is not quickly sold it is there to be browsed over and shared in the informal and relaxed atmosphere of the school bookshop. On average more children browse than buy and to see them reading humorous verse aloud to one another is one of the rewards that makes the whole enterprise worthwhile.

In addition, wily organizers will tempt their colleagues into visiting the bookshop and make sure that a few poetry titles come into their hands, hopefully to be purchased and carried to the classroom. Not enough teachers are seen by their pupils to be buying fiction and reading it for pleasure, let alone poetry. Similarly, unwitting parents can be inveigled into taking popular poetry into the home, for a teachers's recommendation often carries more weight than we appreciate.

The school bookshop can, and should be, one of the focal areas of the school. To achieve this, organizers must also be promoters and their techniques for promoting other books can be as profitably applied to poetry — eye-catching displays, competitions, children's work, visiting authors, home-produced anthologies — all are valuable strategies to bring poetry to the forefront in the consciousness of the whole school community from the lowliest first year to the head, the caretaker, parents, governors and dinner ladies.

Titles worth considering for inclusion in bookshop stock will obviously vary from school to school. However, humour and horror seem to be the most popular. A selection from the paperbacks listed in Appendix B at the end of the book would be appropriate. Above all else it is best to keep enjoyment and entertainment as the basic watchwords: after all, the children are the ones with the money and the power to choose to buy or not to buy!

Poetry and Art

Some suggestions for complementary work in these areas

Lynn Wood

'Where does art come into poetry?' you may ask — there are several different ways in which the two are related.

It is easy to say to a child who has finished writing early, 'Now draw a picture,' but this does not unite art and poetry but merely trivializes both. We know from experience that this results in children racing through writing in order to get to the picture which they enjoy more; or in producing an incomplete and hasty picture in the last five minutes of the lesson. Properly planned, art and poetry can complement each other and lead to a more thoughtful approach to both.

Starting with a Poem

'The Quangle Wangle's Hat'[32] is a poem full of interesting and colourful creatures lending themselves to illustration through collage and model making. An effort to create and represent the creatures in the poem accurately requires careful reading of the details and is one way of focusing attention on the poem. Two other poems about monsters which fire the imagination are 'The Marrog'[33] and 'The Snitterjipe'.[34] They could inspire children to create monsters of their own.

While they are producing their pictures or models they could be thinking about what their creature eats, where it lives and what are its habits or peculiarities. This might lead to poems about their particular creature. Rather than leading children away from the poem after only superficial reading, this approach can lead to a closer look at the original poem. How has the poet described the monster? Does this give children ideas about the monster they are going to produce?

The practical activity of making their own monster often provides them with ideas for later writing. After all, we're asking a lot when we say 'Write a poem about a monster.' Could we do it? The talk which accompanies the making need not be merely idle chatter. For some children telling a neighbour about what they are making can be helpful when they begin writing. They might go on to read other monster poems and make a class collection of their favourites.

With a longer narrative poem, rather than trying to illustrate the poem as a whole it is often more useful to ask a child or a small group to focus on one particular verse or section. This makes the task of illustration easier and helps to focus attention on the words. If a class display is to be made, some decision needs to be made about the size of each picture and common agreement reached, otherwise some of the pictures are out of proportion.

Starting with a Story

It is not always necessary to start with a poem; sometimes a story is a good source of inspiration. I read Tolkein's The Hobbit[35] to my class and afterwards a small group of children made a huge collage of Smaug the Dragon. They produced this very quickly and it was so effective, it stirred up a great deal of interest among the rest of the class and inspired them to write poems about Smaug. They wrote out their poems inside flame shapes and these were displayed around the dragon collage.

Starting with a Theme

It is sometimes interesting to bring poetry into class topics. Last October my class had a Halloween party, and to celebrate this special occasion we spent part of the week in preparation. First of all we found many stories and poems about witches, spells, cats, goblins and other such creatures. I collected some and the children looked in the school and local libraries for others.

We made a huge collage of a witch flying on her broomstick with her cat sitting behind, and this was displayed in a prominent position in the classroom. Then the children made up spells, chants and poems about Halloween to be read on the afternoon of the party. Each child decided what type of creature he would be on the day, and made appropriate props such as cat masks, goblin masks, witches' hats and capes. Some children even went as far as wearing full costumes which they assembled themselves.

On the afternoon of the party, the chairs were arranged in a 'magic circle' and the blinds drawn to add atmosphere. We hung up apples coated with treacle and placed a bucket of water full of apples in the centre of the floor. The children donned their costumes, hats and masks and the party began. Games were interspersed with poems, chants and stories, some read by the children, some by me and some we chanted together. The children were encouraged to read aloud with expression, to add to the atmosphere. The poems and spells were displayed around the witch collage afterwards.

Presentation of Poems

Try to make the children's writing look as interesting and attractive as possible by displaying and presenting it in a thoughtful way. For example, poems about cats could be written on cat shapes; firework poems on bonfire shapes; spells on witches' cauldrons. Good display gives pleasure to the children who have produced the work, and to the readers.

Beware of fireworks and sparks,
Every firework could be dangerous,
Fizzling and spinning through the sky.
All around rockets go zooming by.
Red and yellow sparks fly.
Everyone should watch out.

Joan Barker

I had decided to study the Vikings with a class of thirty fourth-year juniors to coincide with an international exhibition of the Coppergate finds which was being held in York.

For the whole of the previous term all the staff of the school had been consciously encouraging the children to read poetry, giving them time to browse through poetry books, reading poems aloud and using poetry in many different ways. They are very much aware of the value of literature, both prose and poetry, not only for the emotional development of the child but also as an imaginative and linguistic stimulus in children's own writing. They are sure that the greater the variety of styles of writing that the child comes into contact with, the greater will be the chance of him or her developing into a fluent writer. Favourite poems had been chosen by staff and read in assembly for a week, so that the children became familiar with a wide range of poetry from that of Kit Wright and Michael Rosen to Ian Serraillier, Robert Bridges and John Masefield.

Early in the planning of the Viking project, I came across a poem by Gregory Harrison — 'Night Attack'.[36] It tells the story of a young man looking back over twenty years to the night when, as a child, he saw the village where he lived destroyed by the Vikings. It was an unsuccessful raid for the Danes because, although the cattle and young girls were captured and carried off to the ships, a sudden squall drove the boats on to a reef and all were drowned. The boy's father was killed but he and his mother escaped.

The poem describes a Viking attack, but I felt as I read it that much of it could relate to any period of history:

> I was a child that night
> But twenty years
> Have not clapped muffling hands
> About my ears.
> The black hooved rumble of the smoke
> The yellow snarl of flame
> The bubbled plop of resin boiled
> On blistered doorway frame.

This extract has a contemporary ring about it. It could describe tragic human loss in any period of history.

I decided to see what the class could make of the poem by themselves. I split it up into eight story episodes and the children worked in groups of three. They were given time to discuss the poem and were set the task of answering the following questions:

    (i)   What is happening in the poem?
    (ii) What has led up to the events described?
    (iii) What is going to happen next?

Each child then took one of the questions and wrote an illustrated account in answer to it. The poem was interpreted in quite different ways. The group who had the opening verses with the line 'The dragon men are in their boats' linked this with the Vikings, although they didn't know that this was to be our topic. Other periods referred to were the last war, the industrial revolution, a modern spy chase, the Fire of London and a dream fantasy. The group doing the Fire of London took the trouble to research the facts and wove them into their story.

I followed this work with the story of the attack on Lindisfarne as the beginning of our project. At first they linked this with the poem but then, after looking for evidence of the events, decided after a lot of discussion that it was not describing that particular raid as there was no mention of stolen wealth or fleeing monks. Also the first attack on Lindisfarne did not end with the ships being sunk. The children then illustrated the poem to go with a tape recorded reading. I didn't expect there would be any immediate influence on their writing but I have noticed in later work the use of phrases or styles which seem to be in the spirit of the original poem.

> The fiery furnace crackling
> A sword still hot is handed to the warrior.
>> by Graham — in a poem to celebrate a Viking sword.

> Monstrous shadow of the night
> A shuddering laugh surges in his throat.
>> by Edward — a poem about Grendel.

> There is sorrow in our town today
> The children are not playing.
>> by Neil — a poem called 'The Dead King'.

> Solemnly she sails
> Carrying the burden of a dead man.
>> by Fay — a poem she wrote called 'Windlapper' describing a Viking funeral boat.

Twelve Ways of Making Poems

Different ideas for encouraging children to write poetry
which are adaptable for various age ranges

David Bennett

Alliterative Poems (or tongue twisters)

1. Write the numbers 1-5, in words, down a page.
2. Leave a space after each number and then add to each a noun which begins with the same sound.
3. In the spaces include an adjective which also begins with the same sound.
4. After your noun add a verb and follow that by an adverb.
   (If possible use dictionaries and discover less common words.)

N.B. The same can be done by substituting forenames for the nouns. These look good on posters with illuminated first letters and are great fun to record.

    e.g.   'Day-dreaming dreary Debby Dawdles Daily'
            'Bossy beautiful Betty bashes boys'

Acrostics

1. Write the word that sums up your theme down the left side of a page e.g. RUBBISH, BLINDNESS, CITY RUSH HOUR.
2. Each line now begins with the letter on the left. Be sure to keep to the theme and try to ensure that some lines 'swing around' to the next one beneath.[37]

> e.g. **B**oats toppling over every
> **O**bstacle in the current,
> **U**nprepared for boulders in your way.
> **L**oud and deafening crashing rapids
> **D**ashing water rushing in all directions
> **E**normous crashing waves
> **R**oaring water gushing over stones.

Simile Poems

1. Divide the page into two with a vertical line. On one side pupils write a list of six given images, e.g.
   (a) An old lady, dressed in black, knitting
   (b) A spiky cactus nestling in a bowl of gravel
2. The pupils write six companion images that are on a matching theme on the other side, aiming to match the originals as descriptively as possible. (Finding the nouns and then making sure that each has an adjective companion is a good ploy.)

   e.g.

(a) An old woman dressed in black, knitting	A withered spider, weaving its silken web
(b) A spiky cactus nestling in its bowl of gravel.	A tired hedgehog curled up in decaying leaves.

   N.B. These look well displayed with each of the two lists inside a pair of closely adjacent, symmetrical forms.

Colour Poems

1. In five minutes write down all of the items that are of a certain colour.

2. Write down a list, each line of which begins with the colour, as below. Then complete the sentence with four or five other words, one of which must be a noun and one an adjective:-

   > **Red** is a glistening trickle of blood
   > **Red** is a fat, cylindrical letter box.

N.B. for display — two people who have written about the same colour make between them three cardboard cubes, each in that colour. One has 'RED IS . . . ' written on every face and the other two have a sentence from the list on each face. These can then be 'thrown' like dice with interesting random patterns, especially if several children of one colour throw their cubes together. Alternatively stick each poem as a label on a bottle of appropriately coloured liquid.

Unpoetic Poems

1. Make a collection of objects that nobody writes poems about — plugs, a piece of string, an old tennis ball.
2. Choose an object and talk about it with a friend, What makes it so unattractive to poets? Does it have anything to recommend it?
3. Write a 5-10 line poem on a luggage-label shaped piece of card, and attach that to the object. The two can then be displayed togather and handled by the reader.

Pictures

1. Take an interesting picture (a busy scene works best). Divide it into four, either vertically or horizontally by pencil lines.
2. Study each quarter carefully. What is immediately noticeable in it? Look at the colours and tones. Think about weather, time of day, activity etc. Do any similes come to mind?
3. Compose a poem of four distinct sections that moves from one section to another in turn. (Timed to fifteen minutes only.)
4. Swap pictures with a partner and do same for that one.
5. Compare results and together compose two final poems, one for each picture.
6. Display poems alongside picture.

N.B. The same could be done on the close observation of a face.

Paper Bag Poems

1. Pupils jot down on strips of paper <u>one sentence</u> in response to each of five or six questions put by the teacher on a chosen theme e.g.
    (i) How do you feel when you first enter cold water?
    (ii) How do you feel as you hit the water during a dive?
    (iii) How do you feel after your swim?
    (iv) How does the atmosphere of the pool strike you?
    (v) What is it like to be under the water?
2. Take the strips and cut them into separate words. Put these in a paper bag.
3. Swop the bags with another pupil. By a process of selection and rejection each pupil tries to compose a poem on the theme using only the words in his bag. Discourage straightforward recomposition of the other pupil's sentences.

N.B. These look attractive as words glued onto brown paper bags.

Prose/Poems

1. Re-write a piece of highly descriptive prose[38] as a poem. Special care must be taken with selection of material and how the lines are arranged on the page for the most meaningful effects. Preliminary work in these skills will therefore be necessary.[39]
2. Display your poem alongside the original passage.

Family Sayings

1. What things do you say over and over again? What about your family, friends, teachers?
2. Make as long a list as you can and arrange them into some kind of order e.g. Mum's sayings, then Dad's sayings, then Teachers'.
3. Make a decorated page (like old Victorian framed homilies) and write your sayings down.

N.B. These are fun to read to the class trying to get the exact intonation, stance etc. as the donor adopts.

Family Naggings

Who's she? cat's mother?
All I want is a bit of cooperation.
Don't leave the table until we have all finished.
You will have square eyes watching that goggle box.
I told you to go to bed fifteen minutes ago.
You are not having sweet until you have eaten
                        Your dinner.
Take your shoes off before you paddle upstairs.
You would forget your head if it was loose.
Turn them records down or I will break the lot of them.
Put your slippers on what do you think I bought them for?
I was never allowed to do that when I was your age.
Money does not grow on trees you know.
If I have told you once I have told you one thousand
                        times before.
If you want a job doing around here you have to do it yourself.
You do one job and make another.
This is it you see

Parody

1. Choose a poem with an easily definable rhyme and rhythm pattern and theme. Discuss with the group.
2. Set pupils to write their own parody versions.
3. Display original and parody side by side. A poem which works particularly well is Henry Reed's 'Naming of Parts'.[40]

And This is a Glacier

Today we'll do glaciers,
Glaciers are formed . . .,
them's those clear minty things,
With the fox and polar bear.
In the plutonic Ice Age.

Glaciers form cirques and tarns

that circus was good last night
I wonder if that bear was a man
                    dressed up,
By continuous frost action screes appear
A woman did appear to scream last night,
When that bloke fell from the tight-rope.

There are terminal, ground and alluvial
                    mountains
I haven't been down the railway terminal
                    for a long time,
And that will do for today,
After break some river work . . .
A river's first stage is its youthful stage
                    stage
I'll go down the youth club tomorrow night,
I think I'll get stoned,
"Thank you, John a river's bed
does consist of stones."

by Mark & Trevor, age 14

Haiku/Tanku/Cinquains[41]

1. Explain the conventions and look at examples, e.g.
    (a) Haiku — 3 lines, 17 syllables, 5, 7, 5.
                The bell rang out loud.
                The Town Crier cried 'Oh
                          Yez.'
                The people listened.

    (b) Tanka — 5 lines, 31 syllables, 5, 7, 5, 7, 7,
                Smell the stench of fear
                The cries of murdered animals
                Supermarket shelves,
                Mother moans about the rain,
                And packs death into her bag,

    (c) Cinquain — 5 lines, 22 syllables, 2, 4, 6, 8, 2
                Slowly
                Sinking in the
                distance, until it can
                not be seen, only wreckage
                is left.

N.B. Display in small booklets with Japanese designs and motifs.

Accidentally-on-Purpose Poems

1. Begin in rough, filling in this chart on a chosen theme, e.g.:

(a)	(b)	(c)	(d)	(e)
Two Adjectives	Name of animal (noun)	What is it doing? (verb)	Where? (adverb)	When? (adverb)
A hungry mangy	lion	roaming	on the savannah	at dusk at dusk
A striped, lean	zebra	grazing	near a thorn bush	when the sun is high
A snappy, spattered	crocodile	looming	in the stream	at sunset

2. Make a folder of bright card — a piece 6″ x 10″ folded in half. Make 5 piles of 3 strips of white paper, each 1″ x 10″, fold them in half and staple them into the middle forming a row of strips from top to bottom. When the folder is closed you have the equivalent of 6 pages cut horizontally into 5 strips.

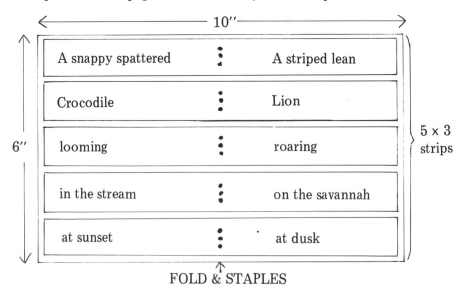

FOLD & STAPLES

3. Write the horizontal sentences from the chart on each alternative page beginning with page one so that column (a) is written on the top strip, column (b) on the second strip down, column (c) on the third strip down, and so on.

4. Decorate the cover and then experiment by turning the strips individually to discover the various combinations that can be achieved — some very silly but fun.
    e.g.   'A striped lean crocodile grazing in the stream at dusk.'

70

Children Talking About Poetry

Joan Varley

Nothing is worse, after introducing a poem to a class, than a stoney silence, when one wanted to develop a discussion. But it can happen and one has to be aware that some classes are better at 'doing' than discussing. However, discussion by the children of their responses to poetry and fiction is important because it is all too easy to saddle them with our adult responses, so concerned are we on occasions to regard ourselves as the handers-on of knowledge and wisdom! Only through being allowed and encouraged to discuss their own responses can children make ideas their own, and develop the imaginative projection into other people, times and places which can do so much to enlarge their view of the world, themselves and their place in it.

Therefore one's choice of poem is obviously important and one's knowledge of the class even more so. Sometimes we can appeal to personal experiences so that all can join in; for example themes on Cats, Pets, School, Jobs and the Family would suit this purpose. At other times a natural lead in will occur with things which crop up in other subjects like Witches, Monsters, the Sea or Transport. Sometimes children need to be lifted above the mundane into the realms of fantasy. But once children do begin talking about particular poems the outcomes are often lively, perceptive, humorous and very rewarding.

One can touch on children's tender spots as I did on another occasion, using the theme of cats and asking about children's individual cats. One child was noticed to be downcast, even tearful. 'Have you a cat dear?' 'Well . . . it was run over last week.' Rather a damper was put on the rest of the lesson as the others comforted her. And yet it did provide an opportunity for spontaneous talk where a child could see the relevance of a poem to her life, and it was something that had happened to her that she could talk about for once, when often she was not able to join in class discussion. Demonstrably, in this instance, the poem was about something 'real'.

The normal approach of 'What do you think the poet is saying . . .?' or 'Why do you think . . .?' and even 'Which words in the poem make you think of . . .?' or 'Can you think of a different ending?' can produce discussion because there is always someone in a class who responds to oral prompting. But sometimes one needs something more than this. A change of approach can work wonders. Pictures, photographs, memorabilia and music are all tremendously useful in introducing a poem, to set the scene or simply to lend atmosphere.

A simple questionnaire, duplicated, and handed round beforehand, helps the children to prepare answers in their minds while the poem is being read, particularly if the poem is a difficult one to understand. One should beware of overdoing this however, lest the sheer enjoyment of poetry is destroyed.

Dramatization of a poem as is described in the account of 'Flannan Isle' (see page 9) can help the children to become closely involved in the poem, so that they are far more able and ready to discuss possible solutions to the mystery of the vanished keepers. The subsequent talk is valuable because of the coming together of children and teacher in the sharing of an experience.

I felt that I wanted to experiment further with talk about poetry with my class of mixed ability nine and ten year-olds. The poetry group had all decided to see how the same poem could be approached in many different ways. The poem chosen was 'Follower' by Seamus Heaney. (For comparative accounts of the teaching of this poem, see pages 45 to 55.) In it the poet describes his changing relationship with his father through the image of ploughing. As a small boy he stumbled across the fields behind his father and the horses; as a man it is his father who is stumbling after him. This was a difficult poem both in its concept of changing relationships and in the technical language used in the description of the ploughing. It was a difficult choice and I led my class very gently into it.

I was lucky enough to obtain some authentic ploughing equipment which made a display in the classroom and after a good deal of discussion, background information and questionnaires I felt something more could be attempted. I decided to let a group of children tape a discussion of the poem and resolved that I would not be present so that they could feel free to say exactly what they liked. As well as being a new experience for the children, I felt it would be valuable for me to see how they worked when free from my direction and how much of this difficult poem they were able to cope with.

It is important at this stage to talk about the factors involved in the organization of such a venture. The first and most obvious point is the choice of the individuals in the group. It is easy for the experienced primary school teacher who has her class day in and day out and who knows them really well to choose a balanced group, to include not too many extroverts, a born leader, a thoughtful child, children with good speaking voices and those with quiet confidence who can contribute orally. In fact a good cross-section is needed. The group was chosen, eight in all, and the equipment was set up in a quiet library. It is necessary to check that the tape recorder is working and that the children know how to use it. They organized themselves very well, and following along the same lines as the class discussion they devised a series of questions which 'an interviewer', who was chosen from the eight, should ask about the poem. He was to ask for each child's views in turn so that each should have his say in an orderly way. I gathered, for I was not there, that they rehearsed this before actually taping it.

It was rather a formal approach and did not produce spontaneous responses from the children, but they had obviously given thought to the method and were taking the occasion seriously. Each person's view was to be heard and respected.

Here are some of their comments. They said they liked the countryish atmosphere of the poem, that they liked hearing about the olden days and the type of ploughing equip-ment used. They really tried and searched for ideas when discussing why they thought it was called 'Follower', suggesting the idea of the son following in the footsteps of the father, that he wanted to be a farmer and that just as he followed the father, then later the father followed his son.

They used thoughtful vocabulary like 'arched', 'muscular' and 'rounded' to explain the 'global' back of the father as he guided the plough. Everyone tried to say something different for 'clicking tongue' — 'directions', 'messages', 'commands', 'encouragement', and 'making the horses go'. At times explanations petered out, but occasionally faltering they maintained the flow and continued. They discussed his 'single pluck' on the reins, saying it meant a jerk, to turn left or right, to tell the horses which way to go. When they came to 'team', one pointed out that it would be a team of horses and not a football team or anything like that. They explained 'eye-narrowing' and 'mapping' the furrows very well, I thought, as 'getting each furrow into line', 'lining it up with something', but when it came to 'hob-nailed wake' they got a bit lost, saying the farmer's boots were 'hob-nailed wakes'!

They seemed to understand the final sentiment of the poem and said the child was trying to do what his father did, and in doing so interfering with the task of ploughing. They voiced the idea that the boy would finally take over the plough, and when his father became old then it would be his turn to follow and stumble behind his son.

I was disappointed at first when I heard the tape because it seemed so formal and stilted, but I realized the very nature of the recording of it made it so, that it had had to be kept orderly by the 'leader' to prevent shouting out, talking together, or shushing each other. They had actually organized themselves very well; they had wanted to keep it clear and easy to listen to, and had become quite adept at using a not very up-to-date tape recorder and an archaic microphone. Their attempts to understand the difficult language of the poem showed a sensitivity and willingness to listen to the ideas of others.

Meanwhile, back in the classroom other valuable talk was taking place. While some children designed templates for doing their own horse brasses another group was engrossed in a quite complicated collage, a scene showing the father and son in a ploughed field. In an outburst of discussion, while some volunteered to make the team of horses, a group of girls discussed the main characters and were busy searching in the fabric or 'bit' box. They had been skilful in their drawing of the father and son and now had to 'dress' them in materials. They talked about what country folk would wear. They consulted Flora Thompson's Lark Rise to Candleford.[42] They scoffed when one child chose a flowered print. 'They wouldn't wear things like that!' What did I think? Had I any more of the corduroy? Would this be enough? Which colours do you think go with this? A cheer went up when a piece of spotted material was found which would serve as a kerchief. A lot of thought, care and discussion went into the collage, until at last they agreed upon fabrics. Paper patterns were made, first of shirts, waistcoats then corduroy breeches, even imitation buttons on the clothes. Sarah seemed to be in charge and gave out the jobs but all in all it was good team work which won through.

This had been another sort of talk, just as valuable and just as worthwhile as the recording, for although the children were not actually discussing particular words and phrases, they had both referred to the poem for details of the setting and characters, and had gone beyond the poem into the atmosphere created by the poet and were enjoying another aspect of the poem, the visual picture created which was something tangible and meaningful for many children. There are pupils who find discussing words and feelings divorced from an actual situation, very difficult, but who can in their own way contribute. It brought the group together in a way likely to develop their own social expertise in interacting and negotiating with others.

The tape recorder talk was thoughtful; and it was a good start and I learned a lot from it. Talk in the classroom has to be carefully balanced. I realized that the child interviewer with his limited experience had not been able to draw out children by asking them further questions. The teacher has a role to play, on other occasions, in leading and shaping discussion, but all oral work should not be managed by the teacher. How can children learn to discuss if they have no opportunities to test their wings? I hope to encourage the children to try a freer format in future, rather than a structured question and answer approach. Encouraging them to experiment with organizing discussion differently will mean showing them other approaches when we work together in class.

This work on tape was very valuable and brought to light problems which I had not been aware of. I could listen and listen again, stopping the tape at any point and be aware of their difficulties and misunderstandings. It provided the children with the opportunity of working in a small group with an end product in mind and produced some very worthwhile work for the rest of the class to enjoy. Bullock describes the value of 'exploratory talk' and the way it can be built on by the very different kinds of talk of a class lesson.[43]

Of all aspects of the curriculum, poetry is one which perhaps does a great deal to promote communication between children and teacher and children and children. Poetry provides one with a golden opportunity of talking for the sheer enjoyment of it, for a oneness with the class, a coming together, instead of 'silent communion with a work card'.

Approaches to Poetry with Remedial, Slow Learners and Disruptive Pupils

David Bennett, Janet Ede, Marylyn Grasar, Joan Varley

Most classes have in them children who may be, variously, remedial, slow learners, and possibly disruptive. The following suggestions are an attempt to bring together the various approaches tried by project members for helping such pupils in poetry work at primary and secondary level. We don't pretend there are any easy answers or sure fire methods for success, but some of the approaches do work some of the time.

In order to help the busy teacher suddenly confronted by a problem pupil we have summarized all the points under 'P' words — rather artificial but we hope some aid to memory in a crisis!

Preparation

This is not so much a method, but rather an approach which is important whatever the method. Some attention, beforehand, to what the non-reader will do while everyone else is searching through an anthology for favourite poems does ensure that all pupils are usefully busy. With some thought it is possible to build up a stock of prepared activities to cater for pupils with specific needs, and these can be used time and again. We have tried to indicate under the various headings where careful preparation, beforehand, of materials and activities is particularly helpful.

Practice in the Classroom

(1) Non-readers, particularly at primary level, can be familiarized with a poem that is going to form the basis of a lesson by being given the poem prior to the lesson as a personal reading book. A series of small poetry books can be prepared by the teacher beforehand, or by more able pupils who enjoy choosing a poem and illustrating it. These books can be used on many occasions, once prepared.

(2) For the non-reader it is possible to prepare a tape with a number of poems on it. A well-illustrated card can be prepared for each poem so that pupils can listen and look at the written version at the same time. We encourage them to listen to taped stories and their reading books, so why not poems? This can be extended by encouraging other pupils to record their own poems and favourites they have chosen.

(3) Artwork of all kinds is not an evasion of the language of the poem. It is an alternative medium through which a response to the poem can be developed and expressed; carefully planned, it can encourage the pupil to focus on the language of the poem.

The writing of shape poems is also an activity which can be made supportive for the slow learner by preparing shapes already cut out in card, for the pupil to fill with words of his own, or words he has enjoyed in poetry lessons. It is important for the slow learner to have a finished product to display at school or take home, and it is up to the teacher to 'engineer' success for remedial and slow learners — success in the relatively short span of a lesson because often such pupils quickly lose interest if the task is too difficult and they see no immediate end in sight.

(4) Looking at a range of anthologies and choosing illustrations which they think partic-

ularly effective for individual poems is an activity which can be done in small groups. An able child can read the poem, and discussion to decide which illustration is most appropriate for a particular poem is an activity in which all the group can join.

(5) The use of a series of cartoon frames to draw the action of longer poems is a method which can work for remedial and slow learners. Each cartoon picture may have just one simple sentence underneath; or a single word in a balloon, which limits the demands on pupil's writing skills even further.

(6) Work on a class or group basis can often support the slow learner. It is possible to show pupils how to turn a descriptive story into a poem by leaving out some of the unimportant words, and then rewriting it as a poem.

(7) For the remedial or slow learner, getting started on that blank white paper often seems an insuperable task. Giving them a formula to write to, such as an Acrostic pattern, is helpful.

(8) Making poetry fun and treating it as a game can also be useful on occasions. Ask the pupils to look at five people. What sort of furniture, animal, car, food, etc. do you see them as? With older pupils this can lead to talk about metaphors. Pupils can read out their ideas and let the rest of the class guess to whom the description refers. Playing 'Consequences' using lines of poetry also has a games element which many children enjoy. Paper bag poems can be fun to create. Write a stock of interesting words onto separate slips of paper. Shuffle them in a bag and let each child pick some out and then create a poem using as many words of the words drawn out as possible. This idea was very successful when tried on a slightly more elaborate scale for 'Poem' by Hugh Sykes Davies. (A number of accounts of this are given in Chapter II, pages 38 to 44.)

(9) Certain poems, such as those with repetitive choruses and chants, can draw out the slow learners, because they can be given a few limited words — even one word — to say with confidence. This approach of 'saying it together' certainly worked in 'Cats' and provided a chance for everyone to experience rhyme and rhythm. Efforts can be taped and questions about the most effective place for a pause, for instance, can lead pupils to reconsider the text of the poem.

(10) The use of musical instruments can be helpful to the slow learner. He can be given a drum, triangle or chime bar, for instance, to accompany the saying of a poem; again this can be taped. The important thing is to let all the children feel they are taking part.

(11) If a dramatized version of a poem is attempted, careful thought on the part of the teacher is required to occupy a disruptive pupil, or slow learner. Simple tasks, straightforward roles or 'star' parts can give such pupils confidence. One particularly difficult pupil was given the part of the lighthouse in 'Flannan Isle' so that complete with torch he was occupied and felt important.

(12) For some pupils oral responses rather than writing poems may be what they can offer most satisfactorily, and a tape recorder can be used rather than asking the pupil to struggle with writing. In some instances it can be helpful to ask more able pupils to act as scribes, and useful pair work can result in such an activity, as the slower pupil needs to listen and explain what he intended. Other alternatives can be found to writing. Asking pupils to think of an alternative title for a poem read to them can be done in pairs or groups. Retelling the story of a poem is another activity which

can help to improve listening skills in small groups.

Presentation

(1) With the slow learner and remedial pupil it is not always easy to remember that it is content that counts, not spelling and handwriting. Insistence on the pupil copying a neat version generally results in more errors and boredom. It can be a tremendous boost to a child to see a blotched page in a beautifully typed version. In primary schools 'jumbo' typewriters make for easier reading. In one school parents were very helpful in giving up a little time each week to typing pupils' work, and it is a way of involving parents in school activities.

(2) It is a good idea to have some very short poems on display around the school. One member in a primary school found that her children liked to read and learn such poems.

Promoting Poetry

(1) Colour coding has now been adopted as a means of organizing books into reading levels. There is no reason why some poetry books should not be colour coded, and it can save a child a great deal of frustration in looking for a book he can read. It is probably wise not to colour code every poetry book, as we enjoy many poems at all ages, and what we are trying to do is expand rather than restrict the pupils' exploration of all kinds of poetry.

(2) If displays of new books in school are being organized, they should include some poetry books, particularly those with good illustrations. The Schools Council research into the reading habits of 10-14 years olds[44] showed that the single most important influence on reading habits was that of the teacher and it is, therefore, important that pupils see teachers reading poetry books of all kinds. Every effort should be made to promote the attitude that adults enjoy all kinds of poetry, even nursery rhymes.

Parental Involvement

At primary level parents are often very anxious to become involved in their child's education and the life of the school. Reference has been made elsewhere to enlisting their help in typing up material for display. Young children can be encouraged to ask their parents about nursery rhymes, for instance. How many do parents know? These can later be used in school for miming, clapping and for work in music. Nursery rhyme books can be used as reading books and are often a welcome change from the reading scheme.

Praise

It is easy to 'write off' the remedial, slow learner and disruptive pupils, and to deny them exposure to poetry because it is considered beyond them, but just hearing poetry can be a spur to an imagination dulled by the utilitarian over-exposure to language drills they are unable to master. The choice of relevant material is crucial and this depends, above all, on knowing one's pupils. Kaye Webb, in her introduction to I Like This Poem,[45] very usefully identifies the kinds of poems which appeal to different age groups.

> Younger ages were charmed by 'funny words' and good rhythms. They
> liked talking animals (cats, dogs, frogs, mice) . . . Nine and ten year-olds,
> while still susceptible to jokes and rhyme, went for more exotic animals,
> and were also more interested in people and places and a spot of action . . .
> Disconcerting but nice to find that 'Night Mail' by W. H. Auden was
> chosen because it rhymes well and is easy to remember.

Our experience suggests that these comments hold true for the remedial and slow learner.
There are, however, pupils and whole classes who are the exception to the rule. One
member describes his surprise when 'Snake' by D. H. Lawrence was a 'hit' with a second
year remedial group in his secondary school! With very reluctant poets he suggests that
it is possible to engineer a way into poetry through other subjects such as art, music and
drama. Placing the emphasis on making a play from a poem or creating music around it,
for instance, can be a relatively painless way into poetry, so that pupils are involved and
interested almost before they realize it.

Using a Library Loan Collection of Poetry Books

Joan Barker

Having decided that we ought to give the children in their junior school where I teach
more opportunity to read poetry themselves, we ordered a collection of poetry books
from Nottinghamshire County Library. Several large boxes arrived containing one
hundred and sixty-three poetry books ranging from out of print anthologies to the most
modern paperbacks. Some were lavishly illustrated, others quite dull in appearance and
presentation, but not in the poetry they contained.

What to do with so many books was quite a problem. We were fourteen classes of
about thirty children each on a split site. I considered that if I split the books amongst all
the classes the impact would be minimal, as each would only have twelve books. On the
other hand a central collection which people could borrow and take to their classroom
would mean that there would be no way of finding out where the books were without a
very involved checking system and the split site would have added a further complication.

I decided, therefore, to divide the collection into five boxes with about thirty five
books in each box. For each box I chose a range of books including nursery rhymes, story
poems, humorous poems and more serious selections. I also ensured that each box contained hardbacks and paperbacks and lavishly and sparsely illustrated books. I made a list
of the books in each box and pasted this firmly to the box for easy checking.

A rota system was drawn up with the boxes going to five different classes who kept
them for four days and then passed them on to five other classes for a further four days.
In this way every class had every book, and because the boxes were only there for a few
days at a time, teachers and children took every opportunity to use the books before they
were passed on. Each new box was awaited eagerly and then long periods given for staff
and pupils to browse amongst the books. Each box was checked by the class receiving it
and at the end of the term not one book had been mislaid.

We agreed that it had been very valuable to have so many poetry books in school and
have now provided sufficient books for all fourteen classes to have a permanent selection

of about forty books.

If you consider organizing such a scheme in your own school it is worth contacting your main County Library to see what they have available. They may have general poetry collections as described above, or be prepared to put together a collection on a particular theme, for a specific age range. It is as well to contact your library service at least a term in advance as the call on their stocks is considerable.

You may also find that new poetry books are on display in your Central Library so that it is possible to see books before ordering for school. Ordering from catalogues is a chancy business. The School Library Service may have librarians available who will visit teachers' centres and schools to talk about new books, and be prepared to bring along new books for inspection. Some teachers' centres have reviewing panels of teachers who consider new books and in some circumstances produce a regular bulletin reviewing new books and their classroom use. It is worth exploring what is available in your area. Certainly we found that the loan of such a large collection in our school gave a boost to poetry reading and very much pleasure to staff and pupils.

Compiling a Magazine of Children's Poetry

Marylyn Grasar

During the autumn term in my primary school I began preparations for the production of a poetry magazine at the end of the school year. I had noticed what a lot of good poems written by pupils were on display in classrooms and corridors and were being read with enjoyment, not only by pupils but by parents and visitors to the school. I felt that it would be encouraging for the children to see their work well presented in print and that it would help to give staff and pupils confidence in what they were doing.

Members of staff usually give back to children any poems they have written that have been part of a display, but throughout the year we collected these poems, together with poems in books and topic folders, so that by June we had sufficient material. There was a last minute scramble to reach our deadline, and one hundred copies were sold within a few days. Almost every family had a magazine, as did the kitchen staff. Since this was my first attempt at such a venture, and also that of my school, it was a case of trial and error, and although the outcome was successful, I could have saved myself a few headaches by planning it slightly differently.

Here are some points which the whole staff needs to consider.

Early Decisions

(1) Will the poetry magazine be a 'grand spectacular' involving several members of staff, or mainly the responsibility of one teacher?

(2) Will it be available for the whole school, one year group, or one class?

(3) Will each child be asked to contribute a poem even if this means including gallant efforts from less-inspired poets?
Will some children have two or more poems included?

(4) I also found it necessary to transcribe some children's poems into legible hand-

writing for the typist to copy. I decided to correct spellings and put in capitals where appropriate because errors in typescript are often a distraction to the reader. However, the urge to correct and improve must not extend to any rewriting of what the child has produced.

(5) As some children will have several poems to contribute, will the child, class teacher, or a group of teachers select the poems?

(6) Will the child's full name, age, or year group be given?

(7) How will the poems be arranged — in themes, classes, year groups, etc? Is there a need for a contents page and/or an editorial?

Production

(1) Ordinary typewriter, jumbo, handwritten? If several people are helping with the typing, layout and spacing need co-ordinating.
Check stocks of carbon paper.

(2) A4 duplicating paper is available in various pastel shades, slightly more expensive than white. Order early!

(3) A slightly thicker front cover would help to promote longer life and a less dog-eared look as the magazine is used. Check that your duplicating machine will take the required thickness of paper or card. Interest in the magazine may be encouraged by having a competition to select the title and cover layout; posters can be designed to advertise the magazine.

(4) The number of pages depends on how you bind the magazine (and whether you print on both sides of the paper or one). Stapling is the easiest and cheapest method of binding. Spines are useful if you think you may need to add further pages later. Spiral binding gives a more professional finish, the pages turn easily and stay open at the required place, but it is difficult to insert further pages later. Some schools are willing to lend their binding machine, and some teachers' centres have them. It is rumoured that some teachers' centres even do the job for you!

(5) How to make up the magazine? Fourth year juniors helped me, and were most interested in the practical aspects of production, but they had difficulty getting the pages into the spine. Fewer children and some parents would get the job done more quickly!

(6) After much discussion about whether to charge for the magazine at all, we decided to charge 15p to cover the cost of materials bought specially for the magazine, and not available from requisition. We wanted to give the impression that we, the teaching staff, considered the magazine worth paying for, but did hand out a few free copies where appropriate. The cost of a poetry magazine at other schools in the area varies from free to 50p. Pupil and parental involvement may be encouraged by announcing that an item has been purchased for the school with the profit from magazine sales.

(7) Methods of selling will vary according to size of school and age of child. All parents were informed in one of our newsletters that a poetry magazine was on sale. Many infants' parents bought it direct from me; it was also available in the bookshop and each classroom.

Two main difficulties occurred when producing this first issue of our magazine. My school is small enough to be able to include at least one poem from each child, which was my original intention, so I was disappointed when I realized that not every child had been able to contribute a poem. In future I shall allow time for checking this and for coping with the problems of duplication. Roneos are temperamental things and school secretaries are busy people. My experience has taught me that I should plan to have the magazine ready about one month before publication day to avoid last minute panic.

We have managed to convince most of the juniors and all of the top infants that they can write poetry, so as a morale boosting exercise it was well worth the effort. Response from parents and children has been such that I am planning another magazine next year, with the hopeful expectation that it is never as bad the second time!

Poetry in the Lower Secondary School

With special reference to 'The Apple Raid' by Vernon Scannell

Trevor Webster

However much pupils may appear to dislike poetry in the course of their secondary education, in the initial years they embrace it with enthusiasm and a fair degree of skill. The reading of poems and — possibly more important — the writing of their own, tends to be an enjoyable and rewarding experience for eleven and twelve year-olds.

The class on which I based my observations was a mixed ability second year, with the very weak pupils withdrawn for extra tuition. The class was generally enthusiastic, willing to experiment and eager to communicate. Our initial experience of poetry writing was the well used and reliable Acrostic, which all children can handle, usually to good effect:

> Gliding through the graveyard
> Haunting the old ruined church
> Owls hoot from the broken tower
> Sightseers flee in terror and fear
> Tremble and twitch as they go.

Having the first letter of each line already chosen offers a supportive framework for writing which many children need, and the question of how much to write is no longer problematic, but clearly laid down from the start of the work.

The Acrostic form can easily be used in thematic or seasonal work, e.g. Ghosts and witches at Halloween, Fireworks and Bonfires on November 5th and Fairground and Roundabouts at the time of Goose Fair, an annual Nottingham event. The essential part of this exercise, in my experience, is that each child discovers the ability and confidence to work with words and achieve some poetic success.

Another enjoyable exercise of this nature, which inspires the imaginative and selective use of words — sure foundations for any form of creative writing — is shape words and shape poems, which may be known to some by other names:

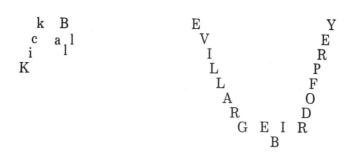

Once again pupils seem to enjoy this sctivity and it serves to develop their experiences of playing with the form and meaning of language.

The class also enjoyed listening to poems being read to them and also choosing poems to read themselves. The works of Milligan, McGough, De la Mare and Michael Rosen were approached and absorbed with eager pleasure. Having created an interest in poetry it is much easier to move towards a close study of specific poems, in this instance 'The Apple Raid' by Vernon Scannell. To introduce the class to his style we read his 'Bonfire Night' and discussed that poem both in small groups and as a class.[46]

For the actual presentation of 'The Apple Raid' the class were divided into pairs and presented with one copy of the poem.

THE APPLE RAID by Vernon Scannell

Darkness came early, though not yet cold;
Stars were strung on the telegraph wires;
Street lamps spilled pools of liquid gold;
The breeze was spiced with garden fires.

That smell of burnt leaves, the early dark,
Can still excite me but not as it did
So long ago when we met in the park —
Myself, John Peters and David Kidd.

We moved out of town to the district where
The lucky and wealthy had their homes
With garages, gardens, and apples to spare
Ripely clustered in the trees' green domes.

We chose the place we meant to plunder
And climbed the wall and dropped down to
The secret dark. Apples crunched under
Our feet as we moved through the grass and dew.

The clusters on the lower boughs of the tree
Were easy to reach. We stored the fruit
In pockets and jerseys until all three
Boys were heavy with their tasty loot.

Safe on the other side of the wall
We moved back to town and munched as we went.
I wonder if David remembers at all
That little adventure, the apples' fresh scent.

Strange to think that he's fifty years old,
That tough little boy with scabs on his knees;
Stranger to think that John Peters lies cold
In an orchard in France beneath apple trees.

After a period of silent reading volunteers read the poem out loud, in the hope that rhyme and rhythm would make some initial impact. The pairs were then provided with a series of questions to guide their discussions of the poem. The questions ranged from the poem's appeal to the senses, a consideration of its general theme and the poet's choice of words, rhythm and rhyme scheme. Each pair was thus able to show some response to the poem. Naturally the depth and range of response varied. The brighter pupils were the ones who attempted comments on the more technical aspects of the poem but each pupil had some opinions and showed imaginative inference. We even attempted to imagine what the poet was like in both character and appearance, which granted wide range to the imagination but at the same time required some critical reference to the text. Their responses to this included the following:

> A mischievous youth.
> A scruffy little boy.
> Lived in a small village.
> Came from a poor background.
> Eldest in a gang and its leader.
> Between eight and twelve at the time of 'the raid'.
> An old man writing memories of childhood.
> Now one of the wealthy living where he used to raid.

After the general discussion, the class were able to talk about their own experiences of scrumping, raiding and general mischief. So the poem was also used as a stimulus to interesting discussion. The final two lines added an air of mystery to the proceedings. Only one pupil suggested that one of the boys had later been killed in war, but the rest made interesting interpretations. Some of the more plausible were the following:

> Killed in war.
> Killed on the front line and buried where he fell.
> Died of a heart attack.
> Wanted to be buried in an orchard — memories of happiness.

Some of the more implausible were two suggestions:

> Choked on an apple.
> Died trying to relive the boyhood exploit of the raid.

However, the pupils did respond in sympathetic fashion to the main body of the poem.

So the final stage was to 'write your own', pooling ideas and technical points from the general discussion. The themes identified by pupils in 'The Apple Raid' — apple raiding, friendship, boyhood escapades, memories and a nostalgic reflection on youth — were good starting-points for their own writing. With this strong rhythm and steady rhyme scheme the poem inspired attempts at controlled verse writing. The class were aware of the limitations of rhyme and in general did not place rhyme before reason. The result was a series of carefully crafted, entertaining poems which covered a wider range of misdeeds.

So the 'exercise' had offered a range of objectives to a group of pupils who achieved some success. The main factors — and the most important — were the enjoyment of reading and writing poetry, and some awareness that poetry is another form of self-expression and not a strange, mystical, or effeminate affair. The lack of success was in promoting deep interest and understanding of technicalities, but perhaps this remains a problem more appropriate to the upper secondary age range. In any case, it is not something which can be grasped by pupils after one lesson.

This group were timetabled for two and a half hours a week of English. When we were working on the poetry project at least an hour a week was devoted to reading or writing poetry. This class did not appear bored, neither did other aspects of English appear to suffer. The discipline of, and linguistic demands made by, poetry can be presented as justification — which sadly is often needed — to parent or colleague alike.

The position of poetry, and its close neighbour drama, is always precarious in the secondary school. The cry of 'What use is it?' can be often heard or hinted at. The basic fact that the first and second year pupils enjoy it is overshadowed in the later years by the pressure of examinations and more directed learning. However, hopefully, the pupils who enjoyed and worked so well on 'The Apple Raid' will continue to respond constructively to poetry.

Presenting Poetry for Pleasure

Jackie Severn

As a non-specialist English teacher, and that for the past three years only, my experience of teaching poetry to children is relatively narrow, and my general view may be considered rather naive. After six years of teaching art, on top of a junior-based training, my aims for English teaching were simply to try to help the children to understand this complex language of ours, and to show them that there was a whole 'world-full' of enjoyment to be discovered in books of all kinds. The inclusion of poetry in my scheme of work seems to be a natural one, and the presentation and illustration of the pupils' own work is made considerably easier by my fortunate position in a secondary school, namely that I have access to art materials and equipment not normally available to the English specialist, and the facility for combining two subjects which, to me at least, seem to go hand-in-hand naturally.

The other main factor in my favour must surely be my personal belief and interest in poetry, for I use it as a valuable and versatile tool, offering pupils the experience of a vast range of situations and emotions. It provides opportunities for creativity, using various media, and is an aid to the enrichment of children's language. I am aware that many teachers are unable to view poetry in this light, having been injured and dissuaded from the subject by the 'poetry-purely-for-passing-exams' syndrome, which was prevalent in our own education. Having survived this syndrome myself, I do consider myself to be fortunate to be teaching English. My art-orientated training, however, stimulates an innate concern that the poetic works which I present to my pupils should be offered in an interesting and aesthetically pleasing manner, where the pleasure is derived from print, decoration, illustration, size, texture and quality of paper, and whatever other enrichments are possible. It also means that I find it vital to allow the children to present their own poetical creations in whatever form they feel is most appropriate. Roney Robinson, in an article titled 'Why Art Teachers should Start Teaching Poetry',[47] suggests that: 'The youngest pupils automatically illustrate their writing, and do so elaborately and without being asked.'

When I begin to teach eleven year-old pupils, I am totally unaware of their previous encounters with poetry, but my concern is the same whatever: that they should all enjoy some form of poetic experience which will make them want to read and write more. It was with this in mind that I suggested to two first year classes that we might make our own 'We Like These Poems' books, having been inspired and fascinated by Kaye Webb's publication for the Year of the Child.[48] As the school poetry resources were somewhat lacking at the time, I made available to the children my own collection of about forty children's poetry books. They spent some time (several double periods!) simply browsing through the books at will, until they each found a poem which particularly appealed to them, for whatever reasons. In order to make our book look as professional as possible, I explained to the children how to make banda masters, so that their contributions could be presented in their own handwriting, and illustrated in whatever way they saw fit.

As expected, the process was long, laborious and often totally frustrating one! There were those who did not appreciate the nature of the carbons, and ended up with smudge marks across their work; there were those who executed the task painstakingly up until the last line, and then made ineradicable errors; and then there were the poor souls who were so overawed by the possible splendour of the whole production that they had to re-start at least three times before they could get beyond the second word of the title! Their reasons for liking the poems had, at my insistence, to be more than "cos it's good!', and so ranged from 'because it makes me laugh' to 'because it is very imaginative', and even to 'because the writer has tried hard to pick the right words to make it rhyme and to make sense in a funny way.' (Spike Milligan!) Finally, however, the time and trouble were made totally worthwhile when each child who had contributed to the book (these being every pupil from two first year classes), was presented with a copy, slide bound and complete. The looks of total enthralment and pride will be impossible to forget.

As a teacher of art, I am fortunate to have my own permanent room, which I can decorate and adorn as I see fit. As well as commercially-produced posters, I have gathered a marvellous collection made by both first and second year pupils. For this purpose, they each had to choose a poem which inspired them to draw a picture, and then to super-impose the poem upon their picture. With some classes, it was possible for me to continue this activity during both art and English timetabled time, but for groups where this was not possible, the process was, unfortunately, a rather long-winded and intermittent one. The illustrations were invented completely by the children themselves, with only two rules to guide them:

(1)   that the illustrations must not be copied from any existing ones,

(2)   that the whole of the paper must be coloured; no white spaces must be left.

When the illustration was complete, each pupil then chose a suitably spaced and coloured area over which to superimpose the original poem, complete with title and author. When the whole thing was complete, each sheet was backed on to a toning coloured background, to complete the poster.

Whenever the children produce any written work in the form of poetry (and this is often their choice rather than my guidance by the second year), I always mount it and group it, so that it may be either presented as an anthology in book form, or displayed as an exhibition of work in whatever part of the school is appropriate. To make this feasible, the books are bound with slide binders, which makes removal and re-assembly easy.

As my concern with children's concepts of poetry has grown, I have tried to find out what they actually think about the whole thing, so I asked a first year class the simple question: 'What is a poem?' In some ways, the question was an attempt on my part to discover not only what their past experiences were, but also what their future expecta-tions were. What I actually did was to present most of them with a task which they were incapable of tackling, because they were unable to verbalise their concept of something which they had never considered as a tangible object. For the majority, poetry was simply a part of everything else studied at school, and not an experience in itself. Some of their

84

written responses however, which follow, I find both illuminating and thought-provoking, particularly with respect to my future handling of poetry in the classroom. Mainly, they make me realise how important the presentation of my own attitude is.

A poem is a Lot of words Put TOGether to make A composition to write somebody a Letter and to write a musical for a Show.

Brian

Most poems have a rythm and make sense but you can have a poem that doesnt make sense

Nicholas

A poem is where a sentence always Starts with a capital letter!

Paul

A poem is a verse or rime made up, by the imaginative treatment of ~~experience~~ expression and hightened use of language more than ordinary speech.

Darren

The poem is the thought and intress of a person who Feels Strongley EnouGHt to wraite about it.

James

Many people do not appreciat good poetry I do not like it that much.

Joanne

Most recently, I asked a new intake of first year pupils to write their own 'First Day at School' poems, having read and discussed a poem by Roger McGough on the same subject. When one girl brought her work for inspection before copying it out, I noticed the writing of an adult in a rough book. Apparently, she had complained to her father that she could not do what I had asked her to do. He had told her, 'If I can, you can,' and had written a poem entitled 'My First Day at School'. I was thrilled at such a response, but afraid that the child's poem might be rather too similar to her father's. However, this was not the case. It was this particular instance which taught me a very important lesson about the presentation of poetry to children. I must share my own experiences with them, just as they do openly with me, and hope that my efforts are as impressive and honest as theirs!

Building a Poetry Pyramid

Teaching towards O-level and CSE poetry in the secondary school

David Bennett

Between my country grammar school years as a pupil and my early days as a teacher the old stage-by-stage course books seemed to disappear to be replaced by the 'topic/thematic' approach to English. I remember only too well the rigid boredom and stultifying predictability and inevitability of the former, and I shudder when I recall my early enthusiasm for the latter, which, as I recall, consisted largely of a witches' brew of unconnected bits that fitted my chosen theme. What I see now, albeit dimly, is that whilst the thematic approach has brought about a splendid liberation in English teaching, we need, too, something of that carefully planned progression of learning and experience that was typified in those ancient course books.

When contemplating poetry we ought not to encourage little else but poetic outpourings from pupils on the topic of our choice, or perfunctory and random glances at poems that happen to fit our theme; then in the fourth year of secondary school hit our pupils between the eyes with our final demand for a lit-crit poetry essay. Most of our poetry work (in fact all literature work) in the first three years of secondary schooling should be following a conscious scheme, forming a kind of pyramid base that makes the final ascent to the public examination summit an easier and more delightful challenge and experience.

My observation is that as a rule the pupils' first O-level poetry essays are enough to weep over and the initial CSE coursework essays on poetry are the first to be extracted when it comes to selection for the final folder. This would seem to indicate that our earlier poetry teaching is not focusing on those things which will help our students most in their later examination work.

Below is a tentative suggestion of points of focus to be considered as a build-up to examination confidence and competence. Poetry writing and poetry reading have not been distinguished one from another, deliberately, for the two are necessary parts of the same process. They are, in my opinion, inseparably related.

For obvious reasons areas of study have not been prescribed to certain years, firstly because one must take into account the ability and previous experience of the children, and secondly because all areas need periodic reinforcement and revision. English departments might well find it worthwhile to work out their own patterns and procedures based upon the suggestions. Basically we should be aiming to guide the pupils in four areas:

(1) to approach the experience of poetry with <u>confidence</u> and <u>enjoyment</u>.

(2) to suggest ways of <u>looking</u> at a poem.

(3) to suggest ways of <u>identifying</u> what has been found.

(4) to provide a variety of methods for <u>recording</u> those discoveries.

1. Activities to Encourage Confidence, Enjoyment and Experience

(a) Encourage pupils to see poetry as a valid and acceptable record of personal experience, emotion, observation and concerns. (This comes best from the teacher's attitudes.)

(b) Provide opportunities for writing about all and everything, for all kinds of audience.

Preferably most work should be often revised and certainly displayed in class anthologies and on corridor walls.

(c) Anthologize on tape or in special booklets, in groups or individually. Children should be encouraged to say or write why they have chosen a particular poem.

(d) Organize taster sessions, including what teachers like – 'Desert Island Poems'.

(e) Provide opportunities for pupils to produce poetry posters illustrating a particular poem.

(f) Emulate or parody a variety of styles.

(g) Deliberately look for the unusual, which breaks from established patterns of writing.

(h) Make poetry books a feature of classroom and library, not occasional migrants.

(i) Poems set to music, illustrated, given sound effects, dramatized.

(j) Choral speaking and learning by heart.

(k) Poetry weeks including visiting poets.

2. Ways of Looking

(a) Deliberately missing off the title on a duplicated sheet often leads to very fruitful suppositions and predictions. (Always ask why each decision has been reached.)

(b) Give the pupils time to discuss in groups and then ask you what they want to know, rather than a teacher-dominated and directed analysis.

(c) Discuss with pupils how a poem should be read aloud before you have done it and thereby interpreted it for them.

(d) Taped group discussions about individual poems can often reveal interesting questions about what a poem means and how it should be said.

3. Identifying Findings

(a) A few basic poetic techniques need to be recognized and practised even if not always correctly named – simile, metaphor, alliteration, onomatopoeia, repetition. (D. H. Lawrence's 'Snake', as well as being a good poem to study, has some excellent examples of the last three.)

(b) Vocabulary and Images – The choice of the most appropriate words and images to express an emotion, character, idea, atmosphere, mood, etc. is possibly easier practised by pupils in their own writing but does need to be identified too, e.g. What ideas/words would be best employed to express the 'owlness' of an owl? Which words and similes express the violent action of water or a bleak landscape?

(c) Lines – Why do they sit where they do on the page?
    (i) Looking and discussing seems to work best with this most thorny area.
    (ii) I have had some success with rewriting descriptive prose as poetry, which proves a useful way to show that poetry is what is missed out! This I followed by re-writing a poem that I presented as prose, as a poem. Comparing and contrasting

the end product with the original helped focus attention on the choice of words and arrangement of lines on the page.

    (iii) Shape poems and acrostics.

(d) <u>Sorting out story from theme</u> — The story can often be represented in cartoon strip. It can be given pre-poem and post-poem additions. I use the word 'theme' to describe that to which the poet wishes to draw our attention or to make us ponder over afterwards. Possibly the best way to deal with this is to discuss and write about the same themes or introduce, deliberately, poems with contrasting themes.

(e) <u>Rhyme and rhythm</u> — I rely heavily on co-operation with the music department. Setting poems to music is very valuable and exploring pop songs can prove profitable. Similarly, emulating standard rhyme and rhythm patterns e.g. ballads, Haiku, Tanka, Cinquains, Limericks. Rewriting 'Jabberwocky' by Lewis Carroll proved one of my most successful forays in this area.

(f) <u>Ambiguity</u> — One of those areas more caught than taught, although I've yet to find a method to 'teach' it anyway! My best advice is to make sure that you have plenty of PUN in your lessons!

4.   Recording the Discoveries

(a) <u>Quoting</u> — Pupils need to be shown how to choose and use an appropriate quotation to back up a point that they wish to make. This is easily done orally and then later work can be structured to show how quotations are effectively set out on the page.

(b) <u>Plans</u> — From the earliest stages children need guidance on how to tackle any essay logically, let alone one on poetry. By the third year my pupils are encouraged to ask themselves:

    What is the story?
    What is the theme?
    What do I see as interesting about <u>the way</u> in which the poet has written it?
    What do <u>I feel</u> about the poem and what the poet is saying?

(c) <u>Comparison and contrast</u> — one of the best ways I have found to stimulate talking and then writing about poems is to compare them directly; how do they compare or contrast in terms of theme, content and style, or else with another poem by a previously studied poet? In a sense this is a coathanger on which to hang thoughts which are to be structured into an essay.

(d) <u>The selection of ideas and the choice of voice</u> — We have all blanched under the onslaught of a string of essays informing us that 'This is a poem with 14 lines, each line having ten syllables, and line one rhymes with line two, and . . .'. I have yet to discover a new and exciting idea to iron this one out. A straightforward session with blackboard and chalk on 'How to Write a Fluent Essay' seems like the very best service we can perform, encouraging and guiding rather than dictating as though from tablets of stone.

To achieve an atmosphere conducive to poetry work in a secondary school, where the mere word 'poetry' does not trigger a universal groan, is a cherished aim for many of us. By taking a more positive and better planned approach, where poetry has become part of a teaching pattern or scheme and not a one-off lesson to be dispensed with quickly, we could reverse that attitude of dislike. Furthermore, everyone in the school would benefit, not just the pupils. The vast store of material and accumulated wisdom and experience waiting to be used and enjoyed is there for us to delve into, to enrich both our English lessons and the lives of all of us. In these ways we might achieve better poetry essays at exam level. Important as that may be, the other benefits that can accrue have an immeasurable and lasting value; the base of the pyramid will remain long after the lofty summit has been eroded by time.

4.   WIDER PERSPECTIVES: THE CLASSROOM AND BEYOND

Janet Ede

If the preceding chapters have succeeded in nothing else, they express the conviction that for the members of the project poetry 'matters'. This was evident throughout our work despite the differing views on the how and why of teaching it. It is understandable that the different ages, temperaments and experiences of teachers should make for diversity in classroom approaches. There are those who have persisted in the face of the indifference of their colleagues in what to some degree is a hostile environment — to some extent they have retreated into their classroom to 'do their own thing'; there are those who feel that poetry is so intensely personal that it is difficult to teach others how to teach it; and there are those who work in a supportive environment where colleagues and children value, and show that they value through their receptive response to new ideas, the 'expertise' of teachers presenting poetry.

Undoubtedly the project has helped its individual members and their schools. Those who have felt isolated in their enthusiasm have met others similarly placed, and have received the support of the group for the work they have undertaken. Those who work in a more receptive atmosphere have been able to work with increased enthusiasm to draw in other staff and children and to make a school occasion of their work.

The practical outcomes of the project are manifest. And yet it is all too easy in a period of activity to be swept up in producing concerts and friezes with equal success, and to fail to ask, let alone answer, the question why? Why poetry?

We each of us develop some views about why we teach certain things. It may be that we are never challenged to make such views apparent, but they are there and, given time for reflection, they can be articulated.

For me this has been the time for personal stock-taking. There has been the realization that much of what I had attempted and achieved as a teacher in school, as far as arousing an interest in poetry went, had led to an excessive concern for our poetic heritage, and an emphasis on the 'great poets' of the English language. Given this emphasis it is easy to see how children's own groping attempts at writing poetry were undervalued.

The project has provided time for me to reflect on the sources of my own conviction that poetry matters, and I go back to the experiences which have shaped this view. They have been varied and began relatively late. While I was an avid reader of fiction in the junior school, drawing on the meagre resources of the large wooden padlocked box which represented our 'library' after the shortages of the war, I can remember no poetry from those days. It wasn't until secondary school that my experience of poetry began — not on the face of it auspiciously. We grappled for a lesson with Keats' 'Ode on a Grecian Urn', and I remember the teacher's encouragement as I struggled to explain to my classmates

'Beauty is Truth, Truth Beauty'. I said the right thing and was complimented on it. What I said is now irrelevant even if I could remember it. What remains of that lesson and another that term on 'Autumn' was the sound of Keats read by an enthusiastic teacher and that is where poetry began for me.

The seminal experiences of our lives may be few and may be barely recognized by us as such at the time. It was not until I began to reflect on my views of poetry and its teaching that I realized that one of the other important experiences of my life was Wordsworth. We read in the sixth form a small fragment of 'The Prelude', in which Wordsworth describes a school friend who had the skill to mimic the hootings of owls so that they answered him across the water:

> At evening, when the earliest stars began
> To move along the edges of the hills
> Rising or setting, would he stand alone
> Beneath the trees or by the glimmering lake,
> And there, with fingers interwoven, both hands
> Pressed closely palm to palm, and to his mouth
> Uplifted, he, as through an instrument,
> Blew mimic hootings to the silent owls,
> That they might answer him; and they would shout
> Across the watery vale, and shout again,
> Responsive to his call, with quivering peels,
> And long halloos and screams, and echoes loud,
> Redoubled and redoubled, concourse wild
> Of jocund din;[49]

This passage was for me a deepening of that enjoyment of sound which had been my starting-point in Keats. Using the resources of poetic language – the play on words, the repetition of sounds, the rhythmic qualities of the language, the compressed imagery — Wordsworth is able to re-create for the reader the echoing calls across shadowy waters as dusk falls.

Wordsworth's strength lies also in his ability to perceive the diversity and yet ultimate unity of the experiences which make up the personality, and to see that all experiences help to shape us:

> Fair seed time had my soul and, I grew up
> Fostered alike by beauty and by fear.[50]

He recounts some of his moments of fear as a child — stealing a boat and the feeling that a huge black shape is pursuing him, and plundering birds' nests on the high crags, where a careless foothold could mean a dangerous fall.

> Suspended by the blast that blew amain
> Shouldering the naked crag.[51]

This awareness of the range of experiences in childhood which contribute to the making of a person says something of the variety of experiences we should be presenting to children: poems, in all their diversity, are one means of presenting children with a range of experiences and the opportunity to reflect on them.

In modern classrooms we are much beset by the neurosis of constantly evaluating the effectiveness of our teaching, and at present teachers are in some ways more accountable than they have ever been — to heads, parents, education authorities, the DES, and other groups in society. Sadly, being human, we seize on the concrete. What can we see has been accomplished? Yet that which we can easily measure is often relatively trivial in its power to explain the effects of teaching on the whole child. As human beings we are infinitely more complex than, for instance, the result of a maths test can reveal, and Wordsworth was aware of this. 'The Prelude', difficult and uneven poem though it is at times, makes this clear. Wordsworth was not a believer in a crude notion of personality which sees it as a result of simple cause and effect. He was aware of the subtleties — of the way in which experiences penetrate the subterranean labyrinth of self and, like an underground stream, wind their way into our hearts to emerge in later life in ways we do not always expect. The mind is not merely a receptacle of experience; it is a shaper of experience.

> Dust as we are, the immortal spirit grows
> Like harmony in music; there is a dark
> Inscrutable workmanship that reconciles
> Discordant elements, makes them cling together
> In one society.[52]

The other side of the coin of measurement is subject matter, a feeling that teaching has been effective when so much information and fact have been imparted. Subject matter, in its narrowest sense, is not what remains of a good education. William Walsh, discussing the education of the teacher, expresses it best when he says,

> Few of us, unless professionally required to do so, could or would wish to recover from the discard into which our minds have thrust it much of the truck on which we and our teachers spend effort, energy and patience at school . . . A good education persists not as a collection of information but as a unit of self, more or less coherent, more or less rich, and a certain method of thinking and feeling, more or less complex, more or less sensitive.[53]

In teaching we profess to have overthrown the crude Skinnerian behaviourism which generalizes about people from a few experiments with ping-pong-playing pigeons. But we have not discarded it in our classroom. Far too often we look for immediate cause and effect. 'He's done the workcard. Now he knows the topic.'

Poetry is not about subject matter. It can, of course, be made to seem so. We can embark on plotting John Gilpin's actual ride from London to Edmonton and Ware and home, by sticking coloured pins in a map. It will not, however, contribute all that much more to our enjoyment or understanding of the poem. Many GCE texts give the illusion that facts are being grappled with in the extensive footnotes which often swamp the text. Poetry is, rather, a form of experience and it offers a means of coming to terms with experience, as Wordsworth shows. Some things are not measurable, and this applies to many of the forms of responses which children make to poetry.

To set a workcard on 'Autumn' would be to test the trivial. 'Can you identify the kind of plum Keats was writing about in his description of it?' is about the level at which we might operate. Poetry is not conducive to the immediate measure of its effect. It penetrates the consciousness subtly. That is why so many teachers are afraid of and even hostile to it. This is no exaggeration. We know, from actual experience, of teachers in utter agonies of apprehension when they see poetry on their timetables. So insistent are they on measuring effect and response that they are unable to tolerate teaching something they may not immediately understand or cannot account to the head for. The only response to some poems is silence. Poetry is one of the few things it is possible to teach without fully understanding it. Nor should we convey the impression to our pupils that there is a prose explanation more valid than the poem. It is possible to teach poetry because we enjoy it. That is where poetry teaching should begin for every child — pure enjoyment, as many of our accounts in Chapters II and III show. Many of us know this is true but we are unable to trust this in the classroom.

Poetry is important in human terms because everyone must, to some degree, come to terms with experience. It reminds teachers that the experiences of their pupils are complex matters. It is important to the pupils because, through their reading of poetry and their own attempts to write it, they are being given the power to work on their own experiences. This is not to pretend that all their poetry will be like Wordsworth's or that every child will, or can be, Wordsworth. At one level the pupils' responses may be an enjoyment of language and play with language — its shape, its sound and its pattern. But through language we have a tool for reflection about ourselves, and this must be given to children to work with. Experiences need not always be first hand to be important. The children's responses to 'Follower' described in Chapters II and III, a very difficult poem for the age groups involved, show just what children can do, if allowed to. They have been able, not just in one classroom, to make the experience their own. They have been able to ask what it means to the poet to be 'a follower', and what it means for them, now, to be 'followers'.

We cannot deny the place of poetry in education when we know its power to evoke such responses as shown in the children's poems. In urging the claims of poetry as a major part of the curriculum we are not asking the schools to buy expensive new curriculum kits at high cost per unit of child.

Poetry is free; it is there for everybody, if we can use it.

Kenyon Calthrop

Not long ago, I found myself in New South Wales driving eight hundred miles or so along red dirt roads into the outback of Australia. It was a strange, almost mystical, experience. Mile upon mile of emptiness with its own extraordinary beauty. The occasional dry, dead tree, a flat landscape, and a horizon so clear and far that it seemed as though the earth's surface curved away in front of your eyes. Rain brought life to the semi-desert and thousands of beautiful yellow flowers appeared by magic all over the ground to flourish and die within a few hours. And not another human being for mile after mile after mile.

But an experience of the outback which I shall carry with me for the rest of my life was not the real purpose of the trip. I was making this extraordinary and fascinating journey to talk about John Donne to the sixth formers of some very remote high schools who had found that this poet was among their Higher Certificate (A-level) set books. So that quite apart from my fascination with the experiences of the journey, I was feeling a very distinct affinity with Evelyn Waugh's character, Tony Last, in the novel A Handful of Dust, who you may remember was condemned to read Dickens to the native population for the rest of his life or to find himself in the cooking pot.

John Donne is probably my favourite poet and his poetry one of the few books which is permanently on the bedside table, so that in one sense I was sympathetic to the task. Yet what was I to say or do? On the one hand a seventeenth century divine, a Metaphysical poet of dazzling sophistication and intellect and on the other pleasant, open, eager children living lives remote from most of the cultural influences of the twentieth century, never mind the seventeenth.

For the differences of time and place, culture and experience could hardly have been greater. What had Donne's complex and powerful intellectual gyrations to do with the actual day-to-day experiences of life on a sheep station in the outback, in areas so remote that, as a matter of course, children were bussed a couple of hundred miles to hear me speak?

There seemed to be only one way in which John Donne might connect with these children's present or future experience. So after dutifully discussing such poems as 'The

Extasie,' 'The Canonization,' 'Hymne to God my God, in my Sickness' and the Holy
Sonnets, I turned our attention to some of the poems which had been very carefully left
out of the 'set' poems, and I finished with an impassioned reading of 'Elegie: Going to Bed':

> Come, Madam, come, all rest my powers defie,
> Until I labour, I in labour lie.
> The Foe. Oft-times having the foe in sight,
> Is tir'd with standing though they never fight.
> Off with that girdle, like heavens Zone glistering,
> But a far fairer world incompassing.
> Unpin that spangled breastplate which you wear
> That th'eyes of busie fooles may be stopt there.
> Unlace you self, for that harmonious chyme,
> Tells me from you, that now 'tis your bed time.

And so on. At least this was an experience with which these children could identify, and
I expressed to them the hope that the first or next time they found themselves in the
situation described, they might perhaps remember John Donne.

Some of the teachers present were clearly not pleased by this ploy (as though John
Donne never actually wrote like that and his passion was solely religious), but at least I had
found one link with outback experience. So I ignored the implied criticism and was thank-
ful that I had not been asked to talk about Chaucer's 'Wife of Bath's Tale' or Alexander
Pope, who also appeared on the list of prescribed texts.

I have recounted this recent experience because it seems to me that it raises a number
of issues which are implicit in some of our earlier contributions and which reflect the
confused state of our poetry teaching. For what are we actually about? Are we concerned
to make our children aware of the great Heritage of Poetry? And if so, on what terms?

The strongest argument for experiencing the poetry of the past is that it can make
children aware of our common human condition — that our forebears had to come to
terms with the same personal problems, difficulties, joys and sorrows we endure. I would
hope that Donne's 'Elegie: Going to Bed' had done just that, whatever the doubts of the
prurient. I am certain that the sense of the past which poetry can give is very important
for children growing up in an age which seems all too anxious to ignore or to distort it.
Yet it must be a sense of the past which focuses on our common human experiences and
our coming to terms with them, rather than a lofty, literary heritage.

For the irony of importing a seventeenth century Metaphysical poet into the outback is the more apparent when one realizes that poetry is still very much part of the life
of the Australian Aborigine — a culture which is strongly rooted in poetry, mythology and
symbol. I was also told of gatherings in the outback where Bush Ballads were sung and
recited for hours. I wonder how many of the children I met had any experience of Abor-
iginal Rain Chants or Bush Balladeers?

Let us bring the argument nearer home. For I do believe that we exist in a cultural
crisis which is less recognized, and more threatening to the common good and the future,
than the economic crisis which is brought so forcefully to our attention. It is the cultural
crisis which makes our poetry teaching confused, difficult and challenging. Denys
Thompson[54] has recently shown very clearly how powerful and necessary poetry was to
the health of the community and how for a long time it was a public rather than a private
activity. But we no longer live in a society in which such public rituals have much place.

I have for some time been concerned at the effect of the decline of religious obser-
vance upon the quality of our language. I am not here concerned to argue whether or not
the decline in itself is a good or a bad phenomenon for other reasons. But what does
concern me is that not very long ago most people were in regular contact with the English